everyday simplicity

Spirituality Books by Robert J. Wicks

Sharing Wisdom

Living a Gentle, Passionate Life

After 50: Embracing Your Own Wisdom Years

Seeds of Sensitivity: Deepening Your Spiritual Life

Touching the Holy: Ordinariness, Self-esteem and Friendship

Seeking Perspective

Living Simply in an Anxious World

Availability: The Problem and the Gift

Self-Ministry Through Self-Understanding

Everyday Spirituality: A Practical Guide to Spiritual Growth

Riding the Dragon: 10 Lessons for Inner Strength in Challenging Times

Simple Changes: Overcoming Barriers to Personal and Professional Growth

everyday simplicity

A Practical Guide to Spiritual Growth

Robert J. Wicks

 SORIN BOOKS   Notre Dame, Indiana

First printing, February 2000
Fifth printing, October 2005
53,000 copies in print

ISBN-10: 1-893732-12-6 (PB)
ISBN-10: 1-893732-14-2 (CB)
ISBN-13: 978-1-893732-12-4 (PB)
Library of Congress Catalog Card Number: 99-67505
Cover design by Maurine Twait
Text design by Brian Conley
Cover photography by Douglas E. Walker/Masterfile
Printed and bound in the United States of America.

Since 1987 I have spent a part of almost every summer teaching at St. Michael's College in Vermont. The response of the students has always been encouraging for me—both immediately after the course and years later when I would encounter some of the graduates in my travels. Beyond this, I have always found, upon completion of the courses, a sense of gratitude to my students for what their questions and comments in class opened in me. I truly feel that my spiritual journey has been changed for the better because of my interactions with the "summer people of St. Michael's College." And it is to them that I warmly and gratefully dedicate this book.

Prayer requires education, training,
reflection, contemplation.
It is not enough to join others; it is necessary
to build a sanctuary within,
brick by brick, instants of meditation,
moments of devotion.[1]

—Abraham Joshua Heschel

contents

acknowledgments

As an author I have always been blessed with editors and publishers who were both good friends and fine professionals. In one sense, what I write is who I am. And so, working with professionals who appreciate my message and help me to present my philosophy in a way that can encourage others to meet challenges, endure suffering, and relish peace and joy in their lives is for me an essential component of the writing process. Without such supportive collaboration my manuscripts would never be released as books.

For years, Frank Cunningham, the Publisher of Sorin Books, and Bob Hamma, the Editorial Director, have done this for me. Together they guided publication of my book on ordinariness, self-esteem, and friendship (*Touching the Holy*), making it my most popular title ever. In encouraging me to develop *Everyday Simplicity*, I think once again they have enabled me to help people find the kind of spiritual supports and guidance all of us need. To John Kirvan, Director of Product Development, who also made invaluable suggestions, I am grateful. He is truly a master of understanding current needs people have and how best to address them in a way that is both practical and powerful.

Stacy Louk, my assistant, was a wonderful support on this project as well. For over seven months she deciphered and typed my script and offered encouragement. Her little note to tell me the manuscript was becoming "awesome" came just when my energy was on the wane. Thank you, Stacy.

To be real, to get to the point, and to share the part of myself that everyone has in common with me, is very difficult. My wife Michaele's reflection on the content, form, and heart of my books always makes this goal of authenticity more attainable. I am always grateful to her, and given the important purpose of this book and the potential good I hope it can do, I am especially appreciative. Writing *Everyday Simplicity* has indeed been a labor of love. Michaele, thank you for adding to this wonderful experience.

where do i begin?

A Spiritual Attitude, Prayerful Life, a Compassionate Presence

---

The one aim this book has is to answer the question: How can I live a simple, strong inner life?

When we think about being spiritual, a number of reassuring images may come to mind:

- A woman gets up before her alarm normally rings. She wraps herself in a robe, walks quietly to a room in the corner of the house, lights a candle before an icon, and sits down for a few moments to center herself in God before her busy day begins.

- A successful salesman who has just completed a presentation to a key client takes the risk of stepping out of his role to mention that the client did not quite seem himself today. Responding to this opening, the client relates the personal anguish he is experiencing due to his son's illness. Later that night, the salesman reflects in his hotel room on this unexpected turn in his relationship with his client, perhaps even the beginnings of a friendship.

- In the middle of the day, a young college student meets a few of his friends in a room on campus for Zazen (sitting meditation). They sit, in a semi-lotus position facing a blank wall, with their eyes half-open and their backs straight, slowly counting their breaths. They leave after forty-five minutes, refreshed, renewed, connected.

These three images all reflect part of what it means to have a meaningful, nourishing spiritual life. But there is more to having a strong, healthy inner life than carving out quiet time for reflection . . . so much more! A spiritual life is developed and deepened when we:

Where Do I Begin?

1. Nourish *a spiritual attitude* underlying all of life which enables us to view *everything* — including our sufferings and confusion — in a way that deepens us and makes life more meaningful;

2. Design "a little rule" of prayer so we can find and nurture a refreshing, renewing place within to be intimate with God;

3. Learn how to share ourselves with others in a compassionate way that mysteriously feeds and enlivens us rather than depleting us or making us feel overburdened and resentful.

There is a beautifully rich Sanskrit word, *visvas*, which is similar in meaning to the English word *faith*. One translation is "to breathe easily, have trust, be free from fear."[2] This describes quite well what we hope to experience at the heart of our spiritual life. Having a sense of freedom from brokenness, alienation, helplessness, anxiety, and feeling totally lost or adrift is a worthy, noble goal. We seek a place within, a vessel, for our passion and peace, where we can go to be renewed and steadied — a place we can also offer to others we meet.

In its broadest sense this is what this book is about — the peace and joy experienced by people who know this experience best called faith.

As a regular part of my summer teaching for over ten years, fifteen or so students and I would reflect for part of the course on "the spiritual life." In 1998, the experience was similar. But, at the course's conclusion that year, I attempted something somewhat different. For the first time, I presented in the last class — in the simplest, most honest, succinct way I could — what I felt were the essential elements of a simple, sound prayer life at the core of a person's spirituality. My goal was to offer in practical, realistic terms a crystal-clear summary of what I believed it meant to have a strong, healthy, deeply-anchored inner life. And in turn, I wanted to make some reference to what might unnecessarily weaken our resolve or cloud our direction in the search for God. In essence, I wanted to offer a logical response to the basic yet profound question: If I want to develop a spiritual life, where do I begin?

In the process of preparing my comments, two hopes guided me. First, that what I said would be a good point of comparison or impetus for the students to develop *in detail* their own spiritual philosophy and practice, what is sometimes called "a little rule." This goal was important because, in the end, each of us must chart a personal, unique path to God within the community of people with whom we travel. As Thomas Merton once said in comparing the spiritual life to the search for a path in a field of untrodden snow: "Walk across the snow and there is your path."[3] No one can give you exact directions. Each person's spiritual geography is unique.

Second, I hoped my structured reflections might help the students avoid undue confusion about their spiritual lives. It is my belief that seeking clarity in how we live the spiritual life is one way to kneel before the mystery and darkness of God. Or, put another way, when we do what *we* can do, we begin to truly learn and have patience with what only *God* can do. Since we often must face the reality of becoming unduly discouraged when we see a spiritual goal but have no guidelines for support, offering simple reflections seemed a good way to encourage people to both begin and "stay the course."

From the smiles on the students' faces and their positive comments afterwards, I was glad

I undertook the effort to distill as much as possible the course's contents. From their reactions, it seemed they felt their notes on that day would provide them a prayerful place to begin deepening their own, unique, continued search for a real relationship with God. The simple summary I provided would assist them to better frame their *own* approach to living life more meaningfully and with greater inner peace.

When I returned home, the presentation and the students' reactions stayed with me. I wondered: Could the same be done for others not present in that classroom? I thought it could. However, I also elected to make two changes to make this more possible.

First, I would need to expand and clarify some of the topics. In addition, I would have to make more explicit three organizing themes implicitly present in the course: namely, the importance of a psychologically and spiritually healthy attitude; secondly, the need for a regular practice of prayer; and finally, the discoveries that a generous—but not compulsive—compassionate life brings. In this way I could more easily organize my comments under these three supports of the inner life: *attitude*, *prayer*, and *compassion*. By doing this I thought it would also be easier for people reading my reflections to use them. And so, with the hope that this brief book may be an encouraging companion for the spiritual journey, it is offered to you as a gesture of support and friendship.

—Robert J. Wicks

Loyola College in Maryland

reading this book

"Is there anything I can do to make myself
    enlightened?"
"As little as you can do to make the sun rise
    in the morning."
"Then of what use are the spiritual exercises
    you prescribe?"
"To make sure you are not asleep when the
    sun begins to rise."[4]

—Anthony de Mello

Everyday Simplicity is meant to be read through the first time in one sitting. My hope is that you will save it for a quiet evening, a cool, crisp morning, or a rainy afternoon by yourself. By reading it in that way you will be able to get an overall sense of what I mean by "having a spiritual life."

Following this, I suggest a slower rereading. Take it with you when some quiet time presents itself. Reread one chapter, sit with it for a few minutes in silence, and then reflect on how it fits in with your own life.

To further encourage this process I have also included a closing quote or scriptural passage as well as simple reflection-questions. These can be made a part of reflecting over each chapter.

As you read this book, I also encourage you use a notebook or personal journal to write your *own* reflections, ideas, struggles, and joys with respect to what I've written. You may wish to include your reflections on the questions and the quotes. Doing this will encourage greater understanding of, and direction in, your own spiritual life.

Following the three main sections of the book are three shorter sections. The first is section IV on "Common Questions on Forming 'A Little Spiritual Rule' of Your Own." This will provide some ideas on how to structure a simple, vibrant, sound prayer life.

Following this is section V, "Relaxing With God: A Month of Reflections, Questions, Suggestions, and Prayers." This part of the book is set up so the material can be reviewed over a period of one month. In offering a line or two to carry with you and reflect on during the day, the aim is to further encourage clarity about your own spirituality.

Finally, at the end of the book (Section VI) is a list of the "spiritual tenets" that close each chapter. Reviewing and learning these little themes will help soften your soul and firm up your resolution to live with greater meaning and prayerfulness.

Seeking as much clarity as we can is an act of respect for God's gift of life. When we open our eyes and stay "spiritually awake," we can be alert to both the subtle and dramatic graces we are offered each day. And that is the purpose of this book, to build a sanctuary within from which we can better sense the gestures of God each day and find a sense of peace and joy that we can effortlessly share with others we meet.

softening the soul

Nourishing a Spiritual Attitude

True ordinariness is tangible holiness.[5]

—Touching the Holy

In reflecting on our search for a meaningful spiritual life, we need to appreciate the attitude underlying it. In seeking to nourish a spiritual attitude, it is worthwhile to ponder the following questions:

How do people feel when they are with me?

Am I really awake, aware, *present* to God in my life *now*?

What does my daily behavior say about the person I really am?

How these questions are answered says a great deal about the maturity of the spiritual attitude which is the basis of our spiritual life. They also tell us about how well we know, love, and share ourselves with others . . . including God. Our spiritual attitude is the soil in which our prayer life grows and from which the gift of compassion is offered.

The search for spirituality doesn't begin in exotic places. Quite simply, it starts within the human heart. The more we are able to discover and be the ordinary persons we were created to be, the more at ease and open we will be to experiencing God's presence each day in life. Moreover, we will receive another indirect beneficial result. In being our true selves we better enable others to find their true selves and God as well. True ordinariness *is* tangible holiness.

For instance, when a young seminarian was challenged to defend a claim he made to others that Archbishop Desmond Tutu was a holy man, he didn't get flustered. He simply responded: "I know Desmond Tutu is holy because when I'm with Desmond Tutu *I* feel holy."[6] Is that how people feel when they are with us? Or, do they feel our neediness, explosive anger, or desire to be right? Do people sense the Spirit flowing through us when in our presence or are they crippled by our need to control, our pressure on them to love us in an unhealthy way, our failure to communicate clearly? Are they overwhelmed by our unrelenting negativity?

How we approach life (our "spiritual attitude") determines to a great extent what we are able to both give and receive. When we are able to let our defenses down we become ordinary, "transparent." Then the Spirit of God both can be *received* and can *shine* through us. Rather than being transparent, we are defensive, filled with ourselves, or we are manipulative charlatans. When our attitude is poor, even if we are "doing good," little of God's love comes through us. For instance, if we give lavishly out of guilt rather than out of love we will feel deprived. In such situations we are so preoccupied with our own image and the tasks we have compulsively set out to do, that there is little energy left to simply be and to receive the love of God. That divine love is present in all situations *if* we have the eyes to see.

Awareness is not possible if our hearts are filled with preoccupation, with the desire to control, or with worry about our image. The beauty of nature and the simple gifts each day brings will go unnoticed if our minds are elsewhere. What happens when we take a ride, walk down a country lane, or relax with a cup of coffee? Do we enjoy the gifts of these moments? Or, are we enveloped with thoughts and worries? Do we really appreciate the experience so that it is daily spiritual bread to nourish us? Or do we come to the end of the lane or coffee break and finally realize we haven't either enjoyed the walk or really tasted the coffee?

Too often our minds are filled with worries or unnecessary concerns. Our hearts yearn to experience God, we long for peace and deep joy each day, but instead we feel lost. A spiritual attitude changes this, it *softens our souls.* It's not that we don't have problems, that we are never defensive or preoccupied. This is part of life. But with the right attitude, things take their proper place.

By being more spiritually sensitive, we are better able to both receive and share God's love. We are in a much better position to be centered and to see possibilities even in the darkness. We are able to receive life's gifts more freely and appreciate many ways to deepen this awareness even beyond times for prayer and reflection. When we are striving to live out a spiritual attitude, our behavior during the entire day is more likely to reflect God's will. And this is very important, because when our will (autonomy) and God's will (theonomy) intersect and are one, we become the person we were meant to be. We are free. We are not captured by the values and fears of the world. Therefore, whatever we can do to nurture such a healthy and powerful spiritual attitude or sense of perspective is essential.

So in order to better nourish a sound and healthy outlook on life which will soften our souls and allow us to experience and share the gift of God in simple ways during the day, the following spiritual themes are worth some reflection:

- Faithfulness
- Openness
- Simplicity
- Gratefulness
- Remembering
- Self-Esteem
- Being in the Now

As we reflect on them, let us once again ask ourselves the questions I posed earlier:

How do people feel when they are with me?

Am I really awake, aware, *present* to God in my life *now*?

What does my daily behavior say about the person I really am?

The responses we have to these questions will say a lot about our spiritual attitude and be true material for reflection. (At least, I have found this to be the case in my own life, as have many others.) A sound spiritual attitude is the fertile ground in which we can cultivate and nourish a simple, strong prayer life and a compassionate presence. With these, we can joyfully greet each new day.

1. faithfulness:

The Portal to Growth

When I visited India in 1998 to facilitate several days of recollection, I read of a contemporary holy man who had gone through many trials. His ordeal was all through the newspapers but I wanted to learn more about what had happened. So, I brought my question to a friend in Jamshedpur. As it turns out, he knew a great deal about the events involved and told me the following story about the circumstances that contained two remarkable tales of true faithfulness.

The holy man in question was a strict disciplinarian in a private residential high school. And so, when he discovered that some of the boys were involved in using drugs after hours in their rooms, he expelled them. For revenge, these boys coerced another young man in the school to claim the man had behaved improperly toward him. Although, the accuser had changed his obviously fabricated story several times when questioned, they still managed to convince enough people to stir up trouble.

The situation reached a pitch when a crowd gathered one night outside his house with torches. When the man finally came out to face them, the crowd forcibly marched him through the streets. They planned to walk him eight miles to the village jail where they would imprison him without a trial.

On the way they were incited further by others who really knew nothing about the situation, but saw an opportunity to join in the frenzy. At one point they shaved the man's head, stripped him naked, taunted him, and hit him with branches as he was marched through the street. Yet the darkness was not to triumph in the end. Because of faithfulness, a light dawned.

First, a group of nuns volunteered to walk to the prison every day to provide him with food. They feared he would be poisoned if they didn't act. Second, poor farmers from his village protested outside the jail until he was released. When a journalist asked how they could afford to do this—especially at harvest time—one responded, "I could not remain in my fields, I could not sit comfortably at my table eating dinner, as long as this holy man who was so generous to me and my people was unjustly locked in jail." They were faithful to him; they demonstrated the value of real community. In this dark time, they discovered spiritual courage that they didn't know they had until this point.

The final and most dramatic story of faithfulness, though, was within the man himself. When he was finally released, he met with a group of people who knew and loved him. When he walked to the front of the room to speak, it was as if someone had thrown a heavy blanket over a blaring radio; the noise of the crowd suddenly became muffled, then disappeared. It was absolutely quiet.

The man then spoke softly but with great conviction. Even people in the rear of the room could feel his strength. He indicated that there was no need to recount his ordeal in detail. The newspapers had in fact covered much of it. But, he said he wanted to tell them something that had happened within him as a result of this:

I want you to know that because of this shameful episode I have lost nothing. They have taken nothing from me. As a matter of fact, actually because of these events, I have become even closer to my God. I know God in a way I never knew before. I have truly found the living God and I am grateful.

Faithfulness opens the door to the spiritual insight that it is not the amount of darkness in the world or in us that is crucial. In the end, it is how we stand in that darkness that really matters. Moreover, sometimes it is paradoxically during faithfulness in the darkness, not in the light, that we may see what is true and dear at a deeper level. At such times, we find ourselves at a crossroads: our spiritual attitude either matures or is crushed.

Faithfulness to God, a deep belief amidst anxiety, sadness, or uncertainty, may not immediately remove the darkness in which we find ourselves. (As a matter of fact, it rarely does.) But, with faithfulness, the darkness itself will eventually brighten and the light of new wisdom for the next phase of our lives will dawn. When we cry out in prayer amidst the darkness, the very circumstances that are so oppressive to us begin to create in us something new. A softening of our souls takes place, we become sensitive to the subtle movements of God in a way that was previously impossible for us.

The lesson: God does not necessarily send the darkness, but within all unhappiness and trauma are hidden special joys and new perspective to strengthen us and offer us new, previously unheard of blessings. For as the holy man in India learned, faithfulness is not only a virtue in the spiritual life; with prayer and perseverance, it is actually a portal to stepping into a deeper relationship with a God who wishes to gently carry us into the next phase of our lives.

For Reflection

Courage comes and goes. Hold on for the next supply.[7]

—Thomas Merton

When was the last time you were in darkness? (Maybe you are in some darkness now.) What helps you not to lose heart? Where do you usually find God in the darkness? What encourages you to follow the teaching of Jesus "to pray always and not lose heart" (Luke 18:1)? How can prayer help you to remember Thomas Merton's reminder?

Spiritual Tenet 1

We are always blessed.

One of the most common mistakes in seeking God in prayer is to stop too soon. Another is to feel God is only present when our prayers are answered in the way *we* want. Instead, persevere, drop expectations, cry out honestly and hopefully to God. Then be open to new spiritual wisdom however it comes. In prayer, while we probably won't get exactly what we desire, God always gives us something wonderful. It would be a shame if we, in our stubbornness, were not to accept this gift and enjoy it at the very time when we are so in need.

2 openness:

Hope in Times of Loneliness

Loneliness and alienation are cogent reminders of how fragile and valuable life is. While our natural response to such experience is to close ourselves in a defensive posture, there is also a way in which these experiences can open us up. This happens when we begin to acknowledge and welcome God in a humble way. At times of crisis we know how much we take for granted, how precious life is, and how easily we can be set off the course we think is so permanent.

Deep loneliness and alienation often strike us at critical points in our lives. Trauma, loss, a falling out with a friend, changing jobs, menopause, sickness, death of a parent, marriage of a child, separation from a spouse, moving to a new home all can trigger a sense of emptiness. Such moments help us to realize that no matter how loving family or friends are,

despite the meaningfulness of work or avoca-
tions, in the center of our lives we are alone and
quite vulnerable. Surprisingly, even little things
like a rebuff from a friend or a temporary set-
back can cause such a recognition.

Unfortunately, loneliness can produce
defensive reactions: greater frenzied activity,
alcohol abuse, a desperate search for new
friends or meaning. It can also induce with-
drawal, anxiety, melancholy, or questions filled
with resentment such as: "Why have people let
me down? Why am I no longer as important in
their lives? Why is life not as much fun or as
rewarding?" At times like this, the questions
may seem endless and purposeless. They seem
to lead nowhere. No immediate answers to our
wishes are produced. People in our lives who
have rebuffed us don't mend their ways and
return to us, with an apology in their hands
and a renewed appreciation of us in their
hearts. No perfect job turns up which quiets all
our questions about ourselves, our relationships, and our work. We feel lost at sea and
nothing seems to soothe or fill the empty ache
we feel deep inside.

How can the loneliness associated with
such transitions soften our souls? What happens at crucial developmental points and crises

in adolescence, young and middle adulthood, and our fifties, sixties, and beyond that can provide new insight and/or solace? Well, once again, there is no obvious, clear path. It's as if we are lost in a dark forest with no light to guide us. While our dominant emotion may be despair, if we can be open to the possibility of hope, something wonderful can begin to happen.

When we feel our heart is breaking or the energy for life is slowly draining from us, if we can see beyond the feelings of loss or alienation, if we can be open to hope, we may experience a softening of our soul, a change of heart, a paradigm shift. And, in that moment, we have an opportunity to experience God and our lives in a new, deeper way. We may appreciate each day more humbly and take less for granted. We may actually notice, in the midst of loneliness and alienation, "the gestures of God who reaches out to us." While the pain of our loss or change will not be less (to expect this is pure fantasy and superficial piety), it will not be without meaning.

What I am speaking about here are the leaps into the unknown that are part and parcel of nourishing a spiritual attitude. The moments or "gaps" of inner alienation occur when the limits of our comfort, pleasure, or understanding are reached. The leap into the unknown is a leap of hope, a hope that beyond comfort lies peace, beyond pleasure is joy, beyond understanding is wisdom. While we sometimes find these gifts suddenly, more often the search requires daily discipline. Without this discipline, or as we'll discuss in the next section, "a little rule," we may miss the possibility amidst the quiet suffering. We can take part in the dynamics of hope if we make a covenant with the living God to stay awake.

So often we sleep through life. If we only snap out of our complacency when struck by a loss or confronted by the fragility of life, any talk about a "spiritual life" will be wistful, magical. There is no magic though.

Yet when we do remain awake, we can sense the gestures of God. Sometimes we can even be awestruck as Jesus' disciples once were.

Jesus took with him Peter and John and
James, and went up on the mountain to pray.
And while he was praying, the appearance of
his face changed, and his clothes became daz-
zling white. Suddenly they saw two men,
Moses and Elijah, talking to him.
They appeared in glory and were speaking of

his departure, which he was about to accomplish at Jerusalem. Now Peter and his companions were weighed down with sleep; but since they had stayed awake, they saw his glory (Luke 9:28-32).

And this awe is available to us when we are attentive, open, supple, humble and, once again, *awake*. From this stance, finally we are able to let go. What we demand of life as a price for our happiness is dropped. We relinquish what has been lost. Even during critical lonely periods, we can open our hands and accept new gifts, new possibilities. This does not fully alleviate our suffering or douse the cold fire of our loneliness or sense of loss. Nor does it eliminate our gratefulness for memory or what we have lost. *But* it does offer a different way of living the short time we have left on earth. It helps us embrace even further what we call "the *spiritual* life."

When this grace is absorbed, we live as we never have before. We pray as if our lives depended on it because finally in the loneliness and alienation that comes our way, we recognize that they actually do.

For Reflection

*Even the predictable turns into surprise the
moment we stop taking it for granted.*[8]

—David Stendl-Rast

David Stendl-Rast in his book *Gratefulness*
says that we leave the house each day with a
mental list of what we will be grateful for in the
day ahead. He suggests instead, throw away the
list and be grateful for the many gifts that we
have been missing in life. What are some of the
ways you can be more awake to the presence of
God in your life and open to the daily gifts you
are being given—even in the loneliness you
may be experiencing now?

Spiritual Tenet 2

Stay "spiritually awake."

This means avoid having expectations of what should happen in life. Instead open your eyes and let yourself be surprised by *all* of life. Such a discipline takes practice. Every morning make a vow to stay awake and remind yourself several times during the day to pay attention to "the now."

3. simplicity:

Space Within

We in contemporary Western society place a great deal of emphasis on security, on having the material, psychological, and even spiritual resources to attain our goals. But in Zen, the focus is not on obtaining something that will make us secure. It is on dropping things so we can have "space" within us where egoism doesn't live, greed is absent, and preconceived notions don't block our clear, appreciative vision of life. While it may be unrealistic to try to create an inner space without any trace of the needy self, we are becoming more aware of the need for inner simplicity. We need an inner sanctuary where the pesky voice of need is quieted and we can simply be. Without such space, we become too distracted and preoccupied to be awake to what is both important and real in life. This simplicity is what the early monks of the desert, known as abbas and ammas, called "purity of heart."

What is the first step toward such simplicity? It is the honesty to see our idols clearly. And what is an idol? An idol is something we make to take the place of God. We know we have made an idol when the possible loss of something or someone creates an inappropriately dramatic reaction in us.

The easiest route to finding out the truth about what our idols are is to look at the feelings we have. What gets us upset? What cheers us? What causes great anger or disappointment? What stresses us out? What drives us or makes us anxious? In other words, what is blackmailing us into believing something must result or someone must respond in a certain way before we can be at peace, joyful?

Naming our idols is important because as long as we are possessed by them we will not be free. Only God can give us freedom. Only the freedom which comes with enjoying the good things in life (family, friends, work, accomplishments, life itself!) as gifts rather than idols can give us peace and joy.

"Simplicity" allows us to be free to both enjoy and let go of all of life because we know there is more; we trust that God will provide us with what we need at each successive stage of life—even after we die.

An attitude like this allows us to be concerned about our family and friends, but not pulled down by them. An attitude of simplicity encourages us to enjoy all we have, but not become addicted to people or things so we feel permanently lost without them. The reason we can do this is that we are grateful for what we have and have had. We trust that all our treasures are from God. While it is natural to mourn if they are lost, letting go allows us to greet new possibilities—even though we might have wanted to hold on forever to what we had.

To reiterate, when our will joins God's will we have real freedom. With this freedom we can enjoy all else that is before us. But when this doesn't take place, we set our hearts on something or someone else. And then in the midst of preoccupations and fears, our highs and lows, we temporarily lose ourselves. To be aware of this basic danger in the spiritual life is worth some time in meditation and reflection. When we recognize what preoccupies us we can also recognize its great—and unnecessary—cost. Paradoxically, an attitude of simplicity also allows us to receive and enjoy more of life than we would if we spent time focusing on whether

we were getting our share. Simplicity trans-
forms us from worried, preoccupied, demanding individuals into grateful "receiving" people.
And, indeed, this is a wonderful grace to
embrace.

For Reflection

*Do not store up for yourselves treasures on
earth, where moth and rust consume and where
thieves break in and steal; but store up for
yourselves treasures in heaven, where neither
moth nor rust consumes and where thieves do
not break in and steal. For where your treasure
is, there your heart will be also. . . . No one can
serve two masters; for a slave will either hate
the one and love the other, or be devoted to the
one and despise the other. You cannot serve
God and wealth. Therefore I tell you, do not
worry about your life, what you will eat or
what you will drink, or about your body, what
you will wear. Is not life more than food, and
the body more than clothing? Look at the birds
of the air; they neither sow nor reap nor gather
into barns, and yet your heavenly Father feeds
them. Are you not of more value than they?
And can any of you by worrying add a single
hour to your span of life? And why do you*

worry about clothing? Consider the lilies of the field, how they grow; they neither toil nor spin, yet I tell you, even Solomon in all his glory was not clothed like one of these. But if God so clothes the grass of the field, which is alive today and tomorrow is thrown into the oven, will he not much more clothe you — you of little faith? . . . Strive first for the kingdom of God and his righteousness, and all these things will be given to you as well.

—Matthew 6:19-21, 24-30, 33

What fills our hearts now and burdens us with worry? Can we see the connection between such worry and idols in our life and the desire to hold onto something that is probably not in our control anyway? Are we able to distinguish between caring on the one hand and wasting energy over what we cannot control on the other?

Spiritual Tenet 3

Make space in your life.

Catch yourself in the act of worrying or complaining and let go of preoccupations and unfinished business which is filling our lives. Let there be room to receive God's new, fresh gifts by appreciating what is in your life *now* and trusting that you will always be gifted in some way in the future. Remember the only thing you can keep forever is God's love. And, when you do try to possess persons and things, you hurt your ability to fully enjoy them while you have them in life.

4. gratefulness:

Receiving God's Gracious Love

I love to visit South Florida and for the past few years I have had an additional reason to visit more often—my daughter Michaele lives and works there. On one visit I commented on the remarkable colors of the evening sky. Privately, I wondered if people there ever got used to the display. Michaele smiled and nodded. Then, after a few seconds, she said in almost a whisper while smiling gently, "Every time I look up at the sky here in Florida, I feel like I am on a vacation with God."

As I was to later realize, this seemingly offhanded poignant comment did not come easily. It was the product of practicing a constant "discipline of gratefulness." Michaele eventually shared with me that on a number of occasions she actually felt quite lost and abandoned by

God. Yet in retrospect she could see and appreciate that "God was telling me something and I wasn't listening, giving me something and I wasn't receiving."

Later, when we spoke again about the beautiful Florida evenings, she honed her spirituality of gratefulness even further for me. She said, "I know the sunsets are for everyone. But as in observing other works of art, what each of us receives from them are personal gifts from God. They are uniquely ours."

There is much we can receive from God if we have "eyes of gratefulness." But if, instead, we face life with a sense of entitlement we will approach life with demands, expectations and rules regarding what we need to be peaceful and joyful. This sense of entitlement is indeed one of the major enemies of a spiritual attitude. It hardens our souls and keeps us from appreciating the gifts we have been given. A demanding nature can even hurt the very people in our lives who may be offering these gifts to us.

How can we confront this danger? The answer to this question is deceptively simple. Receive, don't take. There's plenty for you and me if only we have the eyes to see, the ears to hear, and heart to feel the gifts and presence of God, all around and within us.

Gratefulness

When a member of a leadership council from a wealthy U.S. church returned from a visit to an adopted sister church in Haiti, he was asked what was the most poignant experience he had. "There were so many," he replied. Then after thinking for a bit, he said, "Maybe it was a question one little school girl asked. During a question-and-answer period between those of us from the U.S. and the people of this poor church in Haiti which we were trying to support, one girl asked rather matter-of-factly, 'Do any of the children in your church's school ever go to bed hungry?'"

When I heard him share this, I simply let this question sink in—not just to shame me, though I deserved it; not to make me feel guilty, though heaven knows such a prophetic wake-up call is not out of place with me. I let this little child's comment come into my heart so I could dispel a bit more of my sense of entitlement and increase my appreciation for life and for sharing what I could of it with others. Gratefulness, having eyes of appreciation which open us up to see God's reflection in so many new ways, is at the heart of a sound, strong, healthy spiritual attitude. If we remember this, our lives will begin to change instantly. We will have so much more even during those times when the world would have us think we are poor.

For Reflection

Happiness can only be felt if you don't set any conditions.[9]

— Artur Rubenstein

What often blocks our gratefulness and sensitivity to God are the specific demands we make of people, society, and God. What are some ways we can replace a spirit of entitlement with one of true appreciation?

Spiritual Tenet 4

Receive, don't take.
Recognize that "entitlement" is one of the greatest enemies of the spiritual life. When we have a demanding, needy attitude like this, we waste our energy looking for what we deserve while missing what has already been given to us. It is not that we can't seek more if we feel spiritually, psychologically, or economically needy. But let us ensure that in doing so we don't also turn our back on what we already have but for some reason are not appreciating.

5. remembering:

Recognizing the Continuity in Your Spiritual Life

There is a difference between nostalgia and spiritual remembering. Although there is a certain sweetness to nostalgia, it is but a silver casket when it pulls us into the past so that we can't be in the present. Spiritual remembering, on the other hand, involves gratefully recalling the past moments of epiphany or dramatic awakening in life so that we can muster the courage and perspective to continue seeking God and God's will. Bringing to mind places, people, and times in our lives when we were reminded of the Lord's warmth are indeed acts of spiritual remembering because they encourage us to continue the journey with an open heart.

I can think back quite easily to my adolescence or my early twenties when I was infatuated with God. These moments are the roots of a love which had not matured, so they are important — especially when I feel cold, dry, or distant from God now. When I recall them, it's like I'm fanning embers that are almost cold, but still contain the warmth of those original feelings of closeness to God.

The Lithuanian-American parish I grew up in had moments of pageantry on Easter morning as well as quiet periods of awe cloaked in a veil of incense during evening vespers. Now, whenever I enter a church and smell the settling aroma of incense still lingering in the air, my heart feels warmed. I know I will always be held by a faith community as I was as a child and I am grateful, secure once again. I can clearly recall other moments of warmth, clarity, and peace at other times in different places:

- A fall morning as I walked down a country road in upstate New York;
- At dusk in New York City as I raced through the cold to meet someone for a hearty meal at Gallagher's Restaurant on the East Side;
- The time when I shared belly laughs with my cousin after class in high school;

- At 4:00 a.m. in a quiet candlelit bedroom in India, as I reflected on the scriptures before I had to face the challenges of a new day.

At all of these times, in the recent and distant past, I felt that God was there reminding me of a relationship that was natural, one I wouldn't lose. In these instances, when warmth, clarity, and Presence were near at hand, I knew more clearly in my heart what Jesus meant by the phrase, *"You are my friends"* (John 15).

I recall these words each day as I strive to deepen my realization and appreciation of my real relationship, of a *covenant*, with God. When you use your memory of spiritual encounter in this way it changes you — it enables faithfulness to flow naturally from you. As you remember your history of relationship with God, it reminds you of those times when, although God seemed absent and life had lost its sense of rich meaning, God was there all the while. You no longer take for granted the friendship of God.

For Reflection

God is not always silent, and man is not always blind. In every man's life there are moments when there is a lifting of the veil at the horizon of the known, opening a sight of the eternal. Each of us has at least once in his life experienced the momentous reality of God. Each of us has once caught a glimpse of the beauty, peace and power that flow through the souls of those who are devoted to Him. But such experiences are rare events. To some people they are like shooting stars, passing and unremembered. In others they kindle a light that is never quenched. The remembrance of that experience and the loyalty to the response of that moment are the forces that sustain our faith. In this sense, faith is faithfulness, loyalty to an event, loyalty to our response.[10]

— Abraham Joshua Heschel

In the Hebrew Scriptures we see God's covenant formed with the people of Israel. In the New Testament we experience God's love through the presence of Jesus. The Spirit of God is present the same way today. By recognizing how this has been so in our past, we can stand faithfully in the present in faith no matter how dark or confusing it becomes. What are some of the significant ways you wish to remember how

Remembering

God has been present in your past life? How do
these memories give you strength now?

Spiritual Tenet 5

**Being in a spiritual covenant requires that we
remember God's faithfulness so we don't
ignore our need for loyalty.**

It is essential that we don't let the moments
of epiphany in our lives slip into nostalgia or be
forgotten. They are bright beacons to help us
recall instances of God's love so we can respond
in kind today.

6. discovering your image and name:

Developing a Healthy Spiritual Self-Esteem

Out of "holy remembering," the fruit of a true covenant, comes sound spiritual self-esteem. All of us image and describe ourselves in a particular way. We have labels for ourselves. If they are inaccurate, our image and description can wreak havoc for a lifetime. The sad thing is that most of us don't reflect either on how we view or label ourselves or how those labels are inaccurate and in need of correction. This situation is particularly dangerous because in most cases even fairly accurate impressions still warrant re-examination from time to time. Otherwise, we will live a less than full life. When our self-image is accurate, we grow naturally in our ability to develop and share who we are.

Comparing ourselves to a work of art can be a good first step in the process of looking at how we image or name, and therefore value, ourselves. Do we feel we are like an abstract painting—spontaneous, free-flowing, elegant, and undefined? Or, are we like an intricate Flemish painting whose detailed realism is the product of natural talent brought to the fore through painstaking effort?

By looking at ourselves as if we are a work of art, we will then see how we are defacing or enhancing the gift God wants to give the world through us. If we are organized, we will rejoice in this and catch ourselves when we have a tendency to be rigid. If we are sensitive, we will appreciate this gift while simultaneously checking to see when we are blowing things out of proportion or unduly personalizing and taking to heart comments made by others.

In doing this we then become less defined by how others view or treat us. This can be informative as well if we are discerning in how we evaluate and grow from others' reaction to us. Also, once we have a more respectful, accurate sense of how we are made in the image and likeness of God, we become less needy and more open to being with others in a healing rather than manipulative way. So, once again, we must live and continue to attend to our lives as special gifts from God to us and the world. In this way each new day becomes a true adventure rather than just a place to continue our habits from yesterday.

For Reflection

You must build your life as if it were a work of art . . .[11]

— Abraham Joshua Heschel

How would you describe yourself if asked the question: When you were born, what was the "name" God gave you which best illustrates your unique gift to the world? How are you now defacing or nurturing this gift?

Spiritual Tenet 6

We are God's works of art.
Self-knowledge is a way to find out about God's creation; compassion is a way to share this divine gift with others.

7. freshness:

Being Present in the Now

Too often we think about the spiritual life but don't actually live it. We reflect on past experiences of wonder, read about other people's experiences, or dream about some time in the future when we will pray more deeply. We think, *then* we will experience God in our hearts and be able to share it with others.

The reason this will never happen is: there is no "then." There is only *now*.

The "*spiritual* life" becomes simply the "spiritual *life*" when we begin to see every moment as spiritual. Whether we are eating, sleeping, working, walking, or talking on the phone, we need to be present in the moment and event. Finding God in ecstasy and in boredom, in the kitchen and in the boardroom, requires a widening of our image of God. To do this we need to get rid of a "superego-oriented

God" who is looking over our shoulders instilling guilt. Instead, we need an "ego-oriented God" who is calling us to be all that we can be as people who have been given the precious gift of life.

Sometimes we exclude God because we feel that there will be an air of disapproval if we endeavor to conduct all of our daily interactions in God's presence. Maybe that says more about our view of God than it does about what we are actually doing. A minister related that when he was a child, there was a picture of the Sacred Heart of Jesus in the kitchen. Whenever, he was tempted to take a cookie from the jar that sat on the counter there, he would look at the picture which he perceived as disapproving, and he would resist.

Years later when he told the story to a friend, his friend said: "Oh, I always saw that picture as welcoming and inviting." To which the minister responded: "Gee, I wish I'd have known that back then—I would have reached in the jar and taken two cookies!"[12]

When we are in covenant with the living, loving God, we should be able to break the chains of all the crippling "shoulds" that shackle us, mean-spiritedness, greed, fear, insecurity, habit, and competitiveness. Instead, once the "now" is transformed by God's love for us we experience a new *freshness* to life. This is truly what it means to live the spiritual life here and now, and in every subsequent moment we enter. This doesn't mean we do everything we want or have all we desire. It does mean that we are not tyrannized on the one hand by "shoulds" and reduced on the other hand by induced needs. Instead, we are fully in the moment, experiencing it, enjoying it, neither trying to capture nor reject it.

Paradoxically, people who are able to live in the now are less needy, more giving, less fearful, and more joyful. They are able to enjoy the little things because they are not "little" in the now. They are able to share because they experience more of what is before them and so don't feel so needy.

The problem is that we are trained to prepare for the future, always with an eye to improve our situation, and we are taught to believe that being insecure is only common sense. Simple spiritual living in the now helps us realize that such an approach to life ends in our enjoying very little of it. In many cases, "improving our condition" turns out to be best translated as: "Never enjoying the now until, unfortunately, it's too late." Planning is fine, even necessary. But our lives should not be 95% planning and 5% living. This ratio needs to be reversed so we don't let life pass us by as we are seeking practical measures to improve our lot.

One way to help us break the cycle of forever-planning and never-living is by keeping death in front of our eyes—our own and those dear to us. Just think about people who are now deceased. Wouldn't you like to speak with them now? Don't you wish you had enjoyed their presence more? Or consider this: What if you knew you only had a year or maybe even weeks left? Would you still go through the day on automatic?

Each day I pray that my eyes will be open to the gifts before me. I consciously try to see who and what is in front of me and enjoy these gifts. One of the best ways to "turn back time" in a positive way is not to waste energy on regret or nostalgia, but rather to use past ignorance to help us focus on the sacred, wonderful moment right now. When people do that, just simply that—pay attention to the now—the results are remarkable, especially if this sense of presence allows us to be open to what new things the Spirit of God is teaching us today.

For Reflection

If in the last few years you haven't discarded a major opinion or acquired a new one, check your pulse. You may be dead.[13]

— Gelett Burgess

Meditate on how planning and preparing have resulted in your missing so much of life. Do this until you become so disgusted that you vow to plan 5% and live, fully live, the other 95%. Also, seek to make all things new by having a willingness to "unlearn." Be open to new knowledge rather than being captured by old teachings and experiences.

──────── Spiritual Tenet 7 ────────

Becoming disgusted with how you worry about the past and how you are preoccupied with the future is good — it convinces you to let go and enjoy "the now."

Stop your worrying, let go of your desire to control your future and your erroneous belief that you and the good people and things in your life will never die. Recognize that everything is impermanent. In this way you will appreciate people now, instead of after they die. Enjoy what you have been given rather than greedily holding on; do what good you can now before it is too late. Enjoying the now will help you to unlearn and embrace new knowledge from the Spirit of God rather than seeking the false security of the past.

8. softening the soul:

Some Final Comments

Anne Morrow Lindberg once said: "The most exhausting thing in life, I have discovered, is being insincere."[14] Sincerity truly is the basis of a spiritual attitude that helps our outlook remain clear and hopeful. When we can simply be the person God meant us to be, we can get off the see-saw of inordinate self-doubt and arrogant self-will; we are free, natural. We are transparent rather than filled with the defensiveness, anxiety, and self-gazing that fogs up our vision and makes our lives unnecessarily stressful and driven. We are, simply, ordinary and I deeply believe that true ordinariness is tangible holiness. But being ordinary is not all simple. It requires us to foster a healthy spiritual attitude each day. Otherwise, the simplicity in our hearts will disappear and life will become unnecessarily confusing and complex again.

In this first section the importance of faithfulness, openness, simplicity, gratefulness, remembering, self-esteem, and being present in the now were emphasized as a way to do this. How we view ourselves, God, and the world comprises our spiritual attitude. This perspective determines, to a great extent, how we both appreciate and live our lives. Therefore, sensitivity to how we can nourish and develop this outlook or perspective is essential if we are to live a life marked by simplicity and freedom.

Naturally, what was offered here on becoming more aware and nurturing of our spiritual attitude is just a beginning. There are other ways which each of us, given our personalities and level of development, can also discover as we reflect on this important spiritual and psychological area of our inner lives. In addition, there is more to say about our spiritual attitude in prayer and relationship with others, the two topics we will be turning to now. So, we must be open to the graces we can receive in these two types of encounters as well.

For Reflection

The eye is the lamp of the body. So, if your eye is healthy, your whole body will be full of light; but if your eye is unhealthy, your whole body will be full of darkness. If then the light in you is darkness, how great is the darkness! No one can serve two masters; for a slave will either hate the one and love the other, or be devoted to the one and despise the other. You cannot serve God and wealth.

Therefore I tell you, do not worry about your life, what you will eat or what you will drink, or about your body, what you will wear. Is not life more than food, and the body more than clothing? Look at the birds of the air; they neither sow nor reap nor gather into barns, and yet your heavenly Father feeds them. Are you not of more value than they? And can any of you by worrying add a single hour to your span of life? And why do you worry about clothing? Consider the lilies of the field, how they grow; they neither toil nor spin, yet I tell you, even Solomon in all his glory was not clothed like one of these. But if God so clothes the grass of the field, which is alive today and tomorrow is thrown into the

oven, will he not much more clothe you – you
of little faith? Therefore do not worry, saying,
"What will we eat?" or "What will we
wear?" For it is the Gentiles who strive for
all these things; and indeed your heavenly
Father knows that you need all these things.

—Matthew 6:22-34

What do I feel my overall attitude toward the world is? How can I nurture this attitude so that it is holy, ordinary, and transparent, so that I am more often the person God wants me to be in all situations? What would it take for me to be a more sincere, integrated person with a mature spiritual attitude? How would I look? What are some steps I can take to make this happen? How can I pray each day for the grace to see this as a worthy lifelong quest rather than an exercise in discouragement? How does a truly spiritual attitude set the stage for a simple, strong prayer life? And, once again:

How do people feel when they are with me?

Am I really awake, aware, *present* to God in my life *now*?

What does my daily behavior say about the person I really am?

Spiritual Tenet 8

Seek to be ordinary, transparent, simply the person God created you to be.

Soften your soul by being self-aware so that your defenses don't harden and you become self-involved and protective, rather than self-aware and self-giving. An ordinary person is one who has the right perspective and possesses a spiritual attitude filled with an appreciation for faithfulness, openness, gratitude, and the need to let go of needs, fears, and worries.

forming

"a little rule"

Developing a Practice of Prayer

I never asked God for success.
I only asked for wonder
and God gave it to me.[15]

—Abraham Joshua Heschel

Real spirituality dawns when our life with God becomes as real as the problems and joys we experience each day. Until then we live in two different worlds—one, a seemingly real, practical, and demanding world; the other, a wistful, so-called "spiritual" world. In our daily activities, we may see ourselves enmeshed in the world, perhaps burdened. However, in our prayer we walk in the mystery of God, we dwell in peace, and we wish we could simply remain there.

This separation cannot remain if all our life is to be filled with real meaning, peace, and awe, no matter how violent or stormy our days may become. When we are *truly prayerful* we join both worlds. As we become naturally aware of God throughout the day, we journey in *both* worlds simultaneously. That is truly the spiritual life.

What can bring our two worlds together as one? What can prevent us from being so split that while we are attending to our practical tasks we can only wish we had more energy for attentiveness to God? The answer is to develop "a little rule," a set of practices which broaden and deepen our prayerfulness and may, in the end, enable *all* of our life to become spiritual. The building blocks of such a life of prayer may include:

- silent reflection
- conversations with God
- reading sacred scripture
- faith sharing
- the practice of sacred reading

As we begin to observe the practices of our "little rule," our lives flow in a way that makes everything meaningful and real. Nothing is left out. What is secular becomes sacred and what is sacred is no longer divided from the secular. We begin to feel this in how we welcome everything that happens. We begin to see in a different light what we previously viewed as real and practical, in light of a recognition of our own mortality and spiritual nature. And at this point, all things are indeed made new.

1. enter into silence:

Discover Moments of Intimacy

Each day I look forward to quiet time with God. Even when I'm on the road I take a small candle and icon with me so that when I wake up in my hotel room, I'm not alone or scattered. Instead, with a little icon and burning candle, I can sit quietly with the Lord so my night's thoughts and the desires and worries of the morning can arise, unfold, and dissipate with the flame to God.

In this way, I am centered before going out. Remembering what is really important in life is helpful as I prepare to face others. I am not tossed around by feelings, reactions, rejections, or apprehensions that have nothing to do with what life is truly about.

Silence never comes instantly. We are trained to be distracted (even when we are asleep, we are often filled with noisy dreams). Our days are filled with thinking, telephoning, entertaining, accomplishing. When we stop, the roar takes some time to quiet down. Sometimes the noises settle into one theme (e.g., a confrontation which may be coming up later in the day) that we need to hand over to God. Other times, the noise lessens and we are allowed to just sit warmed by the light of God. These are moments of divine intimacy. It is at these moments that we cease listening for the words of God and allow the silence to somehow teach, comfort, and console us. The silence itself becomes the voice of God in some strange way.

Most of us yearn for this silence especially in the morning and evening. But we have a storehouse of excuses as to why it is not practical:

"My house is too noisy to find quiet."

"There is no place where I can sit for a few minutes in silence."

"I really don't know how to meditate."

"My prayer never seems like that of the people who write about prayer."

"When I sit to pray, I just worry."

"I get good ideas which I get up to write down before I forget them."

"I wouldn't even know where to begin."

"I've never prayed very well except for times when things are bad."

"I just fall asleep when I sit quietly in the morning or evening."

The excuses are understandable, endless, and are still, well, excuses. If we want to enter into a refreshing quiet place within ourselves we will need to have patience and exert some effort. As a matter of fact, such a place is already there within us. We were born with a natural childlike wonder and joy within. With some quiet, perseverance, and a few simple steps, we will see it again in ourselves. Here are a few simple actions that can be a part of your "little rule":

• Find a quiet place in the morning and/or evening where you can retreat for a little silence and solitude. When a quiet place is almost impossible to find in a busy household or small apartment, I have gotten up earlier or stayed up later than everyone else. I've stayed in bed awake, used the bathroom, or sat in a corner with a book as if I were reading. But having a corner or a room where you can go and close the door is ideal. A familiar place without so many immediate distractions helps one to settle down for silent prayer. I find that lighting a candle before a little icon or inspiring picture also signals to me that I am being more intentional about God's presence in my life. It further dampens the distracting noise in my mind and reminds me that life is short and today is my eternity, so I'd better pay attention to the now. Someone once said that "life is something that happens while we are busy doing something else." So, this lighting of the candle is a gentle nudge to wake up to precious time I have been given.

- Sometimes it helps to soften the soul by reading a little bit of scripture or a few pages of spiritual reading. These words are not meant for analysis, but simply as a companion to sit with you, like a friend content and silent.

- If you find yourself worrying and feeling worse in the silence, then stop and turn to a line from scripture or a favorite inspirational book. There are so many to choose from. Christians can take a phrase from Thomas Merton, Hindus can choose a line from Paramahansa Yogananda's book *In the*

Sanctuary of the Soul, Jews can reflect on a line or two from Abraham Heschel, and Buddhists can reflect on the written advice of the Dalai Lama or Sogyal Rinpoche. (A list of books on the spiritual life can be found at the end of this book.) And of course, each tradition has its own sacred scripture. Whatever line you choose, it should remind you of God's love and the peace that is possible when one is not mesmerized with personal faults or the sins of others.

- When it seems that nothing is happening in prayer, patience is important. If you feel extremely distracted, repeating a certain word (love, Lord, gentleness) can help to settle the soul. If you feel like a perennial beginner, remember the words of the mystic Thomas Merton: "In prayer we are always in over our heads."[16]

- If prayer is seen as just another thing to do, another duty, another time to please someone else, it is important to reframe it. Silence and solitude is a time and place to relax and rest in God's arms. It is a time to love and be loved. Even if one doesn't feel this love, the idea of love should be held in mind until it falls into the heart.

This simple advice is meant as an encouragement to spend time in silence and solitude as a way of feeling at ease, loved, and free. As was noted, this book's bibliography contains a list of volumes that are spiritual classics. They are not imposing or difficult works and reading them will support the move to silence where God can speak. In addition, they can encourage us to welcome solitude where we can be alone with God (or one with the world) instead of being caught in a life of grasping, attachment, and painful destructive desire.

For Reflection

When you are faithful in [silent meditation] . . . you will slowly experience yourself in a deeper way. Because in this useless hour in which you do nothing "important" or urgent you have to come to terms with your basic powerlessness, you have to feel your fundamental inability to solve your or other people's problems or to change the world. When you do not avoid that experience but live through it, you will find out that your many

*projects, plans, and obligations become less
urgent, crucial, and important and lose their
power over you. They will leave you free during your time with God and take their appro-
priate place in your life.*[17]

—Abbot John Eudes Bamberger
speaking to Henri Nouwen

Where will you find a place to sit in silence
and solitude, wrapped in gratitude? What
would interfere with your taking out a few minutes to be by yourself? How can you deal with
these potential blocks?

Spiritual Tenet 9

Each day move to a refreshing and renewing place within, a place where you are in silence, solitude, and wrapped in gratitude.

Set aside at least two minutes of quiet time for perspective to take root in the morning. When this can be longer it will be wonderful, but it should never be absent—even when you are busy. Always take at least two minutes to stop and center yourself. Return to this interior place during the day and for a few minutes in the evening if possible.

2 conversations with god:

Open a Window to Heaven

Conversations with God are our "windows to heaven." I hope that in today's technological society, we haven't become too sophisticated to have them each day. I find that such discussions teach me, keep me honest, and help me in the search for perspective and peace.

Once I was asked, "What part of our conversations with God are merely a projection of our own thoughts?" In other words, "How do we know what is from us and what is from God?" My answer is simple: I believe *all* of the words in our conversations with God project out from our own thinking. And yet, what God is saying to us is still in our words, our thoughts. However, it is up to us to try to discern within those words, those conversations, what is from God and what is from us or our conscience. With this challenge in mind, I believe the *source* of the messages we hear in our "conversations" are best discerned not by trying to uncover "divine words" but by looking at the *fruits* of our prayerful conversations. The real measure of our conversations with God is in the ordinary, the daily.

If we feel energized or challenged by our conversation rather than depressed, unduly anxious, or stressful, then the themes we arrive at probably are more inspiration than delusion. However, even after recognizing this we should still bring themes of discernment to people we trust. (As the saying of the early fathers of the church cautions: "Whoever is his own spiritual director has a fool for a director.")

Two additional steps that can make our conversations with God richer are (1) honesty, and (2) efforts to move away from speaking with a "superego-oriented God" to speaking with an "ego-oriented one." The first point about honesty is self-evident, though not so easy. In prayer, I ask people to just blurt out to God whatever they are feeling and what they believe God might be saying to them. Just let it flow — wait until later to sort out what you really believe is from God. In this way, we can get around the tendency to censor or fool ourselves in a particular way. Who knows, if we do this we may even be able to be more honest with God than we usually are with ourselves!

The second point probably needs more explanation. By "superego-oriented God" I mean: the image we have of God which comes out of our conscience—especially when that conscience is a harsh one. Too often our conversations with God are short-circuited or skewed because of the narrow fabricated god with whom we speak. The themes in such instances are guilt, demand, rejection, and obligation, and the voice is parental (in a bad sense).

The "ego-oriented God," on the other hand, is the God who calls, loves, encourages, and challenges us. Rather than using just our conscience, God primarily uses our heart. Rather than the voice being negative, the language is love. This does not mean we are given the message: "Anything goes." The scriptures would never justify this. Even scripture contains messages of prophecy which instill some guilt to wake us up. However, there is a sense that while occasional guilt may be needed to push us to do what is right, the spiritual life cannot be sustained in this way. Love continually encourages us to do what is right because it is what is most natural for us.

So in conversation with God, expect love, feel love, know love before you start. Then, just let the conversation flow. Share your strong feelings and then let God speak to you.

Again, once you have themes you feel are from God, think about them. Pray over them in silence and share them with a trusted guide. This will lead to an experience of God that will both nourish and intrigue you. It will set the stage for a more real and intimate relationship with the living God — and isn't this what we all seek?

For Reflection

If you have deep devotion for God, you can ask Him anything. Every day I bring new questions to Him, and He answers me. He is never offended by any sincere query we put to Him.[18]

—Paramahansa Yogananda

What are the most important things going on in your life now? Share them with God before you go off to work. Also, at the end of the day let God know how your day was and offer thanks for the preciousness of life.

Spiritual Tenet 10

Converse honestly, openly, and often with God each day.

Help your prayer relationship become more natural and deep by speaking about the little things that happen to you and the specific big concerns you have. Bring your questions, feelings, confusions, and your love to God. Simple flowing conversations let God become part of your day.

3. appreciate scripture:

Touch the Holy

I am always surprised by how little time most of us spend enjoying sacred scripture. Relaxing at night or in the morning with the word of God is such a beautiful way to nourish our lives and avoid an unanchored prayer life. As we read the words of others who have walked before us, we see the relationship God has with us today. When we read it for longer than a few moments, we venture into an appreciation of God that is not possible to sense when we just read or hear little snippets read to us in the church, temple, ashram, or synagogue.

All faiths have their "sacred texts." Whether it be the Upanishads, the Koran, the Hebrew

Scriptures, the Bhagavad Gita, the Good News of the New Testament, the Psalms, or other words which have come down to people of faith through the ages, it is essential that we not turn our back on the foundation of our faith.

When we take these writings and picture ourselves in the stories, when we reflect on how we would act and interact, we become part of the stories which formed others. They begin to shape our destiny as well. There are many dangers that come from not reading sacred scriptures. Faith often becomes rootless, God becomes vague, and in times of crisis, we feel especially lost. A simple commitment to reading and relaxing with scriptures for at least fifteen minutes each week will be transformative. As we sit with scriptures during, or at the end, of a stressful week, our troubles and confusion don't disappear. But, with the sacred words before us, our concerns take their proper perspective and move to the edge of our lives rather than remaining as tyrants at the center.

This sense of perspective becomes possible when we see that we are not alone. We feel as the authors of the psalms did when they cried out in their troubles, looking for a sense of acceptance and solace from God. Scripture helps diminish the distance between God and us because we can become part of the story. Ironically, scriptures are not irrelevant because they were inspired and written in the past, rather, they are eternally relevant because they help us see beyond our current frame of reference which may have trapped us. Too often we can't see beyond our present situation—a situation which in just a few years, months, maybe even minutes, won't be the same. Scripture reminds us of this eternal wisdom, it offers us support and helps us remember the place of God in our lives.

For Reflection

He who seeks an answer to the most pressing question, "What is living?" will find an answer in the Bible: Man's destiny is to be a partner rather than a master. There is a task, a law, and a way: the task is redemption; the law, to do justice, to love mercy; and the way is the secret of being human and holy.[19]

—Abraham Joshua Heschel

What is your favorite passage from scripture? Begin reading scripture for fifteen minutes or so each week. Underline the passages that strike you and write them out in a little spiral notebook, which can be your own heart of sacred scripture which you can look to for support and encouragement in times of trial and joy.

Spiritual Tenet 11

Sacred scripture breaks the chains of contemporary thinking, so we must read it as often as possible with a sense of spiritual freshness.

We must not read it as if we know the stories and are just going through the motions. Instead, there must be hope, fervor, and intellectual interest about what this "old friend" will say to me *now*.

---

4. share your faith:

Create Quality Time

Whenever I am with a group of people—in class, or in church, in a restaurant, or at a meeting—my feeling at a very deep level is, "This is my community. These people are my family." They are with me now, in the present. I feel the same about persons with whom I journey as a mentor. Even though they are not family or friends from the neighborhood, they are special to me in a new and different way.

This attitude has helped me to relax, to be open more quickly to their gifts, and to feel free to share mine without wasting effort on whether I'm liked or well received. I have also begun to appreciate the "ordinary saints" around me—people who are holy and especially gifted by

God but who are not recognized yet by society. In a way, that's all the better since society seems to associate sainthood with the spectacular, and then tries to show that the person has clay feet, in order to deny the value of what they have just praised!

If we welcome others with openness and hope, with minimal categories and expectations, we can be the recipient of wonderful insights. We can celebrate the temporary in ways which will bring epiphanies to open up each day. Unfortunately, though, the converse is true as well.

Recently, there was a meeting of church administrators in Baltimore. Nine people were invited and I knew about four of them, two of them fairly well—one was a bright, talented administrator, the other a quiet, gentle professor who has a sense of understated holiness. After hearing the results of the meetings, I realized that they, more or less, accomplished what they needed to do. But from the comments of one of the participants it was obvious that my friend the administrator got into the task, pushed forward his agenda forcefully, and in the process missed seeing and drawing strength from the holiness of the professor. The thought I had was: "What a shame." Then, I wondered: "How many times have I been like this man, dismissing the holy because I had my own agenda and a narrow, fixed view of what was truly holy or not."

I think we must find our invitations to community everywhere, and be attuned to faith-sharing opportunities with groups of new and old friends as they present themselves in ordinary situations (at dinner, in the hallway) and without the use of religious words. With such an openness, you may be surprised at how different, enduring, and nourishing faith-sharing groups spontaneously develop.

Once on a drive up to Philadelphia to have dinner with a group of Catholic religious sisters, I found myself smiling and really looking forward to the situation. (I consider Philadelphia home because of my wonderful years there and I have always enjoyed the company of these sisters.) Yet, when I thought about it, I realized that in some unusual way, I believed I had more in common with them and religious sisters at a Carmel in Baltimore than I had with some of my family or fellow professionals. This seemed strange to me since I saw them so infrequently, until I recognized that they were searching in faith with a sense of hope for the same things I was; we had a philosophy of living, an ethos in common. Being with them, I felt my spiritual journey was encouraged and nurtured, which is important if I am to continue "to fight the good fight" and not give up hope. Faith-sharing opportunities are essential elements in a deep prayer life.

For Reflection

We can take a lot of physical and even mental pain when we know that it truly makes us a part of the life we live together in the world. But when we feel cut off from the human family, we quickly lose heart.[20]

— Henri Nouwen

Who comprises the circle of friends that challenges, teases, supports, and spiritually nourishes you? How can you arrange to spend quality time with them in person, by phone, through letters or e-mail? What are your hopes with respect to these relationships? What contributes to the constructive nature of these relationships? When are they destructive? What is your role in this and how can you improve the quality of the encounters? (i.e., How can you accept people where they are, set the stage for them to be all they can be, and not put expectations on them which are unreasonable?)

Spiritual Tenet 12

We need a faith community of friends to inspire, challenge, tease, and call us to be all we can be without unduly embarrassing us for being where we are now.

Insure you have people you can see, visit, call, write, or e-mail who will nourish your spiritual life. Be careful of those who would laugh at, belittle, or subtly erode your faith in God; they probably are ignorant, not malicious. Remember, whether I drop a rock on your head on purpose or by mistake, you still get a bump. Be wary of being with such people.

5. practice sacred reading:

Lectio Divina

Reading is wonderful. It has the power to entertain us and the power to help us see the truth in a new way. Reading can rescue us from living too narrowly. Life is short, after all, and reading helps us see the daily possibilities that often pass without recognition.

"Sacred reading" does not so much describe the content of what we read, but the way we go about it. Sacred reading can be done with scripture and books about the spiritual life, but also with biographies, novels, and other genres as well. We can enter into sacred scriptures by imagining ourselves within the stories. We can do the same with biographies, or with journals carrying to us a real sense of journey. We can be transformed from armchair adventurers into active participants when we read with a sense of expectation.

No matter what I read, I have a pencil nearby to mark off passages that I think are important (actually, since I'm so obsessive-compulsive in my approach, I also have a ruler to underline each important line!). I do this with all books, even novels. What I underline could be a story, a turn of phrase which breaks through my shell of complacency, or a principle or practice worth noting.

After finishing a book I review my underlined sections to see if I still feel these passages are important. If I do, I copy them out by hand under the title, author, and publisher of the book. Doing this, which is a time-consuming chore, ensures that I only copy what is really important. If you are like me, in the beginning of a book you may find that you copy long passages. But as you get into it, you become more and more discriminating.

After doing this, I review these pages and immerse myself in the themes and try to absorb the spirit which they contain. Following this I may underline part of the quotes themselves and write key passages again on index cards. I do a great deal of this work so I can absorb into my consciousness what I have discovered with the hope that it may become part of my philosophy of living. Also, to aid this, I read more extensively in certain areas or with individual authors so I can appreciate the depth and development of their thinking.

I view this unique approach to reading as my own brand of *"lectio divina"* — an ancient monastic practice of reading, reflecting, praying, and contemplating the word. (There is a fine introduction to *lectio divina* by Basil Pennington in the listing of books on the spiritual life.) It opens my heart to a broader way of seeing, a deeper appreciation of other people's lives, and a greater sense of God's movements in life. Reading then, when it breaks open the shell of my quiet ignorance, helps me feel like I am living alongside God.

For Reflection

Fine biographies give us both a glimpse of ourselves and a reflection of the human spirit. Biography illuminates history, inspires by example, and fires the imagination to life's possibilities. Good biography can create lifelong models for us. Reading about other people's experiences encourages us to persist, to

face hardship, and to feel less alone.
Biography tells us about choice, the power of
a personal vision, and the interdependence of
human life.[21]

—Matina S. Horner

Given your schedule and reading style, how can you structure your day/week so reading sacred scripture and other nourishing books is more possible? What would you feel comfortable doing (underlining, taking a few notes from what you have read) which would help you better absorb the messages God may be giving you through what you read?

Spiritual Tenet 13

Absorb good messages from sacred scripture, spirituality books, and other types of reading.
Do this by underlining in the text, copying out important quotes, and even inserting yourself in the story imaginatively (especially in sacred scriptures). "Feel" the important themes within yourself.

---

6. gently develop "a little rule":

Some Summary Comments

In the spiritual life there is always a tension between structure and spontaneity between personal discipline and inner freedom. In this section, the suggestion was made to gently develop "a little rule" for ourselves, a framework so life doesn't slip by without our sensing both the gestures of God and the preciousness of a life lived with sensitivity, gratitude, awe, and compassion.

Silent reflection, conversations with God, enjoying the heart of sacred scriptures, informal and formal faith sharing with others, and reading in such a way that our souls are immersed in themes that both awaken and deepen us were suggested as ways to form such a framework. If these approaches turn into just more things we should do, they will fail. If, on the other hand, they are ignored and we just float through life without seeking to provide ways to ensure spiritual sensitivity, we run the danger of missing our own life's meaning and objectiveness.

To strike a balance between an approach to prayer based on duty and a life without prayer, we need to incorporate prayer practices into our lives that we want to engage in because they are invitations to greater joy and peace. A little rule developed by us should be balanced, enticing, truly nourishing, and challenging. When it is, life changes (maybe imperceptibly at first) and becomes filled with a sense that the spiritual journey is a journey that we can both appreciate for ourselves and share with others by fostering simple compassion. Can you ask for more than this?

For Reflection

To learn meditation does not, therefore, mean learning an artificial technique for infallibly producing "compunction" and "the sense of our nothingness" whenever we please. [It] means to gradually get free from habitual

*hardness of heart, torpor and grossness of
mind, due to arrogance and non-acceptance of
simple reality, or resistance to the concrete
demands of God's will.*[22]

—Thomas Merton

What would a vibrant prayer life look like to
you? What elements from among the ones covered would you include in the development of
"a little rule" of prayer? What would be the one
step you would like to take next to deepen your
prayer life? . . . Well then, if it really means so
much to you, take it.

Spiritual Tenet 14

**To have our spiritual life give structure to our
day, we need to develop "a little rule" of
prayer and reflection.**

In this way, rather than letting our lives slip
away or inadvertently move in a direction we
didn't want to go, we can stay both disciplined
and alert to the presence of God in all of our life
experiences.

completing the circle of grace

Fostering Simple Compassion

It is in the shelter of each other that the people live.

— Irish Proverb

A young man about to be ordained a priest received a book by Henri Nouwen from one of his friends. He took it with him on a retreat and was particularly struck by one sentence in the book. Since he was artistic, he decided to look in the woods for a rock upon which he could paint the line. It would be a personal return gift for his friend, who was also approaching the time of ordination.

As he walked around looking on the ground for the right rock, another retreatant spotted him searching and asked if he had lost something. He looked up, said "No," and told the passerby the story of what prompted the search.

Smiling, the stranger replied, "Well, I'm Henri Nouwen. *Let's look together.*"[23]

To "look together" for God is a perfect description of compassion. Compassion is not a matter of giving compulsively and lavishly. Instead, it is the natural outgrowth of having a spiritually-rounded attitude and a life of prayerfulness. But such a life of compassion is sometimes not easy.

Being a compassionate person can be exhausting, frustrating, and a seeming waste of time. Sometimes when we are trying to be helpful we feel like the donor in a blood transfusion, as if life's energy is being pumped *out* of us. We wonder: Where will I get the energy to survive, much less be compassionate? When we are immersed in a terrible or dark trauma, there is a slow draining of our hope and our passion. Life becomes a tired color of gray. Paradoxically, it is often in those very moments of "grayness" that we can finally reach out to others in a natural, rather than compulsive, way. It's as if our exhaustion has broken down our compulsiveness and we are free to be ourselves. When this happens we experience not exhaustion, but the exhilaration of a new perspective. When compassion joins an attitude of awareness and the practice of prayerfulness, "a circle of grace" is formed. And, at the center of this circle is self-knowledge, healthy self-love . . . and *love of God*.

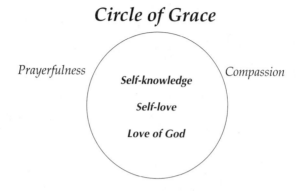

Circle of Grace

Prayerfulness — **Self-knowledge** / **Self-love** / **Love of God** — Compassion

The circle of grace is the place where the presence of God in us meets the presence of God in others. From this interaction, what is important is revealed, learned, and then shared. The circle is dynamic, so grace is received in different ways, again and again. With humility, this knowledge becomes wisdom. With compassion, the essential wisdom becomes love. And with love, all things become new. In other words, compassion is the essential activity which helps ensure our prayer life's vitality, reality, and meaningfulness. It may even enliven our faith when it is flagging. Once when the German theologian and mystic Karl Rahner was approached by a young man asking for books to help him strengthen his faith, he surprised him with the answer: "No books. Instead, go out and help the poor of Munich."[24] It was in *compassion* that he felt the man would find the answers to his spiritual questions and doubts.

Sometimes, on a really down day for us, maybe there is little we can do for others. But even in those instances, if we keep the value of compassion in mind, we may at least know enough to keep quiet instead of saying something unkind. Maybe we won't be much of a help, but at least we won't be a pest to others. Keeping compassion always before our eyes completes the circle of grace. The spiritual life finally becomes so real that it has a chance to "positively contaminate" all of life, all of the time. Then, life as a whole becomes spiritual — which is our ultimate goal, isn't it? In this light, fostering simple compassion is not only reaching out to others, it is also an act of prayer which welcomes God into our soul in new, mysterious ways.

1. living a life of nobility and involvement

The heart of compassion, the chief fruit of prayer, is *nobility*. Abraham Heschel aptly described a life in which the circle of grace has been closed: "What I look for is . . . how to live a life that would deserve and evoke an eternal Amen."[25] Yet, a life that includes sharing ourselves with others in a meaningful way is too often short-circuited by a sense that the problems of life are too overwhelming. We feel, in down moments, that our efforts would bear little if any fruit. Or, that in the process of helping, we would be completely overwhelmed ourselves.

In moments like this, I have recalled the words of a physician working with starving

Somalians. When asked how he could continue to face such despair and human horror and challenged to explain how he could continue to be involved despite the odds, he simply replied, "You can't lose hope as long as you're making friends."[26]

People are not noble because they succeed or are applauded by others. Their lives are honorable and worthy of emulation because they are striving for what is good—no matter what the results! God asks us to be involved not because we are called to be successful, but because we are called to be *faithful*. Moreover, this very act of faithfulness, no matter how little the impact appears to be, teaches us lessons in perspective and hope which can only be taught by acting compassionately.

In many circles today, nobility is seen as unattainable. Being pessimistic is in vogue. Being hopeful is not. In the media there seems to be a process going on to support this negative cycle. It is the search for heroes who are then debunked as charlatans.

Often, those who are doing some good in the world are uncovered and at first praised—praised in a lavish way as if they were "gods." Then, in the spirit of investigative reporting, their foibles are uncovered and much ado is made of their clay feet. The harm done by this process is manifold. Included in it is the message: "There are no really noble and good people in this world. All of your idols are phonies. You are, therefore, a fool to believe in anyone or to think nobility is attainable." What a shame it is that some of the media and many of us do this to wonderful, but human, people who are only trying to do a little good in the world. They didn't ask to be cast as saints, and they don't deserve to have their faults spotlighted nor to be viewed as charlatans.

Once someone said to me, in the spirit of this prevailing negative feeling, "Why is there so much evil in the world?" In response to the discouragement in the voice of this fine loving man, I replied: "Instead, I find a greater question is, 'In the midst of all the real evil in the world today, why are there so many good people still performing healing acts?'"

The seeds of nobility are present in our world, in our community, in our family and friends, in *us*. Each day, no matter how many times we fail, this must be remembered, believed, and followed as best we can.

I once said to a group of persons in ministry: "You give me courage. It is not because you are perfect. Since my specialty is working with helping and healing professionals, I know better. You are human and in doing good you fail at times. And so, when I drive past your field hospitals, community centers, schools, rectories, and convents, I am inspired *not* by your success. Instead, I am enlivened by your courage to commit and recommit to what is noble, what is good. That is what I hope would inspire some people when they look at me as well. We are all in this together as people seeking a life that we hope will evoke an eternal Amen as we honestly recognize the daily sins and foibles of which we are guilty." The cornerstone of our compassion then needs to be faithfulness. We must seek God in the very process of being a balm for the sadness, loss, and fears others experience.

For Reflection

The problem is why my child should revere me. Unless my child will sense in my personal existence acts and attitudes that evoke reverence — the ability to delay satisfactions, to overcome prejudice, to sense the holy, to strive for the noble.[27]

—Abraham Joshua Heschel

What in us enables us to continue to strive to live noble lives? What are the daily dangers in ourselves and the world which threaten our commitment to be faithfully compassionate? How can I actually draw energy from being compassionate rather than just expend it?

Spiritual Tenet 15

Living nobly is not just a worthy goal, it is an act of worshipping the God who created us to present divine goodness where everyone can take heart from it.

In the heart of each person is the possibility to bring the love of God to others in a unique way — whether they notice, appreciate, receive it or not. Being faithful to the desire to act in a way that allows this to happen is our daily way of honoring God in public.

2 offering balm for tears in the souls of others

As a generally happy person I am always surprised at how easy it is to have little events crack the dam of my sense of joy and empty an apparent reservoir of sadness into my day. It seems that there are permanent tears in my soul which reopen so easily that part of me steps away from the experience and actually marvels at it.

During these times I have learned important lessons about myself. It has also helped me be more sensitive to others. We are a fragile race. Small rebuffs and little failures can easily and quickly turn days and weeks into very gray periods. When we recognize how easily we can be hurt, we tend to seek to be more gentle with others.

Beyond little rebuffs and hurts, trauma (e.g., sexual abuse, death of a child, a serious loss, injury, or accident) can dramatically affect a person and derail them for years. Complicating matters is the difficulty we sometimes have in reaching out for help. Sometimes we do it in ways that keep at bay the very people who could best stand by us.

People who have suffered serious deprivation early in life also may have difficulties in being heard and cared for. Though trying to do the right thing, they may come across as angry, misunderstood, ungrateful, explosive, and needy. These are the very people who need a listening, sensitive ear despite their unpleasant manner. But this is not easy and we must listen with compassionate ears. When they say we are not doing enough for them—even when you've walked the extra mile and then some—they are really saying: "I'm in a panic because no one seems to be able to soothe the depth of my pain." When they say: "You don't understand" (even when you've spent more time and effort than any other ten people trying to do just that), they are really saying: "Your efforts at understanding have still not relieved my pain; I'm worried that you don't see the awful state I'm in right now."

The type of balm for tears of the soul that we can offer varies. For some, just listening is enough. With others a little feedback is needed. Some require both our attention and some limits on our availability so that they learn to deal with reality and don't wear us out as they have other people. But in all situations we need to offer some of our joy and peace through attention, listening, concern, some problem-solving help (if they ask), and a willingness on our part—and this is important—not to look for gratitude or an indication they are following our suggestions. We must receive our satisfaction from our faithfulness alone and not from results or gratitude.

Patience and a willingness to be with others are true balm. By letting go of the need to achieve results or appreciation, this kind of solidarity with people can bring much grace for both parties. If we are spiritually awake, the person with whom we share a little of our happiness will somehow help us see God's grace. This can only happen if our "eyes" are not clouded over with our own needs for immediate gratitude or for a breakthrough of some sort. That is the spiritual mystery of compassion. As we seek to welcome others, we find our lives are changed for the better as well, if we are prayerful, rather than compulsive and fearful.

For Reflection

I have spread my dreams under your feet:
tread softly because you tread on my
dreams.[28]

—W. B. Yeats

Faithfulness and a recognition of our own limits are two important lessons to keep in mind when we are compassionate. How can we be more faithful? How can we set limits without feeling guilty or taking offense when a needy person gets angry at us or shows us they are let down when we don't give them as much as they desire from us? How can we practice opening our eyes to the presence of God in very difficult situations, rather than looking only for the divine presence in gratitude, positive results, or indications that a person is following our guidance?

Spiritual Tenet 16

Offering balm for tears in the souls of others as a way of making God's gentle presence known in the world requires us to remember two important elements: our limits and our need to be faithful no matter what the results.

3. welcoming home:

Real Hospitality

Just before Christmas of 1998, I walked around the house with its lights and decorations, paused, and felt very grateful. Not for my possessions — though I had been blessed with many of them. But for the warmth they symbolized.

In this spirit, at that moment, I called my daughter in Florida. I told her that I was very happy she was coming home for Christmas. I said that when she came home, I hoped she would feel the presence of God in our little house. I told her that the house with all of its decorations was wonderful. Yet what really would make it special was being together as a family, to experience "home," and know what being gathered in the name of the Lord really meant.

A number of years ago when we prepared to move to Maryland from West Chester, Pennsylvania, I realized more clearly what "home" was about in a simple encounter. We had our house up for sale for about three months when a middle-aged but newly married couple came in. They loved the house immediately and offered to purchase it. When I asked them what they liked about it, the man mentioned some of the neat features of the house while the wife stood silent, smiling slightly. I turned to her finally and asked, "What about you?" She looked around at the shelves of books and the small arched fireplace and out the sliding glass door to the back deck. Then she sighed, and said almost hoarsely, "The peace I feel here."

This sense of peace is the real hospitality we need to offer people when they come into our lives, our "spiritual homes." Whether it be a chance encounter in a hallway, a long talk on a park bench, or a quick phone call, people must feel they are being welcomed home; they must feel the peace of God. They must feel the ordinariness, openness, and welcoming spirit that comes from an attitude and life of prayer and gives them the room to be and explore themselves further.

Hospitality is not simply being "chronically-nice" to strangers. Instead, it is offering others a gentle space where they can feel welcomed for who they are now. To do this we must have such a space within us—one that has been cleared by a recognition of our own sinfulness and a belief that we are forgiven and called to go on with what new knowledge we have learned about ourselves. Thomas Merton put it simply: "Admit your mistakes, then move on."[29]

People can sense when you've been honest, forgiving, and compassionate with yourself. They then take the courage to be that way with you . . . and themselves. Such a process is tentative at first but in the long run quite healing. Sometimes I am not the one to see the results, but at least I seek to be part of the process, as many people in my life have been with me.

Those who are judgmental and somewhat rigid or jaded about people are often failures when it comes to being welcoming. Though they don't want to be, they are "prickly" even with those they know and love. They recognize how their harshness hurts but don't seem able to stop themselves from providing a corrective comment or judgment, if not out loud, at least mentally.

This spontaneous negative style, in which anger or disapproval rises naturally and easily to the surface, needs to be replaced and softened with a little daily attention and care. But it must be done on a *daily* basis, without the self-defeating fantasy of permanent change. It also must include a willingness to tease and laugh at ourselves when we fail—which we surely will since we are human.

First, we must take the effort to see how we are welcomed home. We can do this by appreciating God's boundless love for us even when we err. In the Christian New Testament we see Jesus' compassion for Peter, the thief hanging on the cross, the woman about to be stoned— fairly dramatic stuff. But also look at all he was willing to endure in the apostles on a daily basis: their jockeying to be first, their conflicts and doubts, and ultimately their fears and ambivalence. Is it any wonder that he lamented he had no place to lay his head? Yet, isn't it even more of a wonder that he never abandoned them? He remained faithful until even Thomas who doubted him and Peter who ran from him returned with hope.

We need to echo Jesus' actions as well as the forgiving spirit of people like Martin Luther King, Jr. and Desmond Tutu by welcoming ourselves in the same way. If there is a primary way we should be like God, it is in the power to forgive ourselves.

In line with feeling welcomed by God and ourselves, we are then in a place to welcome others. This needs to include the people closest to us: our family, friends, and co-workers. This is often difficult because they feel they "know us" and often unconsciously undermine our efforts to be welcoming. Such kindness, warmth, and efforts at positive change are sometimes met with low-level resistance. People are unnerved by change—even for the better—because it may call them to alter their style as well.

Once when a young man was on retreat he reached the insight that he needed to be kinder to his parents. When the long weekend was over and he returned home, he took the little step to begin the process by saying "thank you" when his parents did something for him. After he did this twice, his father looked up at him when they were at the table, smirked, and said, "Oh, so a few days away on a retreat, and now you're holy." The boy was so embarrassed that he gave up his resolution, feeling like a fool for having made it in the first place.

There is a happy ending, though. Later on in life he was to reflect on this episode when once again he was derided by a family member after choosing to do something good. This time he was able to recognize the fear in the other person and was determined not to be derailed by it. He recognized that God welcomed him, took an effort to gently be hospitable to him, and recalled the faces of people in his life who through the years have encouraged him to grow.

This last support is one we must not neglect. Friends who foster our spiritual life can help us weather the storms of rejection and misunderstanding. In my own work, I have made so many mistakes and have had so many people key in on these errors in character and judgment. Hearing the awful (and unfortunately usually true) assessments people have made of me has been devastating at times. Literally, some of the comments I have heard about myself have brought me to my knees.

At times like these, supportive friends and prayer have helped me appreciate more and more that only my image has been hurt by such comments and reactions, and in the end, it is best to let go of that anyway. Hopefully, it has also made me a little more compassionate toward others, which is the best outcome of small and large sufferings.

Suffering can make us hard. It can result in a gray outlook on life, punctuated only occasionally with joy. It can lead to sadness or depression. It may upset us so much that we want to run away from it, compartmentalize and wall it off, and find pat, predetermined ways of explaining it. Or, it can, in the end, make us kinder, more welcoming people. This is not only a beautiful gift to others, but is also a wonderful way to be with ourselves and with God.

For Reflection

Compassion is hard because it requires the inner disposition to go with others to the place where they are weak, vulnerable, lonely, and broken. But this is not our spontaneous response to suffering. What we desire most is to do away with suffering by fleeing from it or finding a quick cure for it.[30]

—Henri Nouwen

Do we offer people a gentle, open place to be themselves and tell their story? Are we able to be open to God's love and a sense of our own spiritual self-esteem so we can share it with others? Can we really welcome people home?

Spiritual Tenet 17

Real hospitality is not merely being nice to people we don't know; it is welcoming them into our "home-with-God" through gestures which help them to find the divine presence in their own lives.

To do this we must replace our spontaneously negative style to feel anger, annoyance, mistrust, resentment, and alienation with understanding, acceptance, joy, love, and peace. Of course, all of this takes great practice and is the outgrowth of a sound prayer life.

---

4. performing simple acts of kindness

Kindness is simple, profound. It doesn't take much time, yet leaves a lasting mark. As I look back over my life I can easily recall so many people who were gentle and good to me. Some are gone now — it is too late to thank them personally. However, I can do better than offer them my words of gratitude. I can emulate them with the people who are in my life now. It takes so little effort most of the time.

On a visit to Cedar Rapids, Iowa, I heard about a cardiopulmonary surgeon who was a legend in the hospital among the patients and staff. He was an excellent surgeon, but that was almost a given in this hospital of fine physicians. What he was known for beyond his technical expertise was his visible kindness.

Although he was very busy—in many cases busier than some of his colleagues—he approached his patients with an aura of "I have all the time in the world for you." He would come into the patients' rooms, sit down, stretch out his legs, and inquire after their health. He usually didn't stay very long, but it felt like he would stay for hours if needed. Patients felt cared for and at ease. He was present to them.

He was the same with the families. You would occasionally see him perched on a windowsill, leaning forward toward a family member with his chin leaning on his hand, listening intently. He saw both the family and the person who had surgery as worthy of the highest attention. He was not only competent; in a word, he was "kind."

Kindness requires slowing down, paying real attention, and sharing some of yourself with others. But that requires you to get out of yourself, your own needs, your own desires. Actually, because it is a product of our gratefulness to God in prayer and is cradled by our spiritual attitude, kindness is unselfconscious. If you feel you're being kind, that's not real kindness. Kindness is a natural unselfconscious outpouring of all you know you have been given yourself. That is why people with seemingly little can be so kind. They have the good fortune to feel blessed in all they receive, so the blessings keep coming and flow through them to others.

Two elderly women taught me this lesson clearly and set out in sharp relief two dramatically opposed models—one to follow and one to avoid. One of the women, Janice, was dying with cancer in a hospital. A generous woman of simple taste, she was friendly, caring, a good listener, and had a wonderful sense of humor. Her friend Jo was very needy, self-involved, always complaining and looking for sympathy, and never really happy even though she had so much.

When I called to tell this perennially unhappy woman that her friend had been diagnosed with cancer and it didn't look good given her tests, she was momentarily concerned. Then as if a switch had been thrown in the conversation, she changed the topic to her own arthritis and the discomfort she was in.

Rather than seeing this as a sign of the woman's great neediness and her inability to truly be concerned about anyone other than herself, I saw red. Out of my grief, I said: "I just told you about Janice's cancer and you're telling me about your arthritis?" To which she responded: "You just don't understand."

She was right, of course. I didn't understand. I didn't have the openness and generosity to recognize how sad it was for this woman to be in such an ego-involved state, not to be able to be compassionate for her own dying friend. Even when she did reach out, you had the feeling you would be better off if she hadn't!

The story is not over, though. Later that week I went to visit the woman with cancer. As I came into the room, she was sitting quietly by herself, propped up with pillows. When she saw me her face lit up with a smile and a touch of pain.

"How are you?" I asked, for lack of anything better to say. "Fine," she said. "Are you comfortable?" I asked. With a puzzled look on her face she said: "Do I look comfortable?" I laughed. She was too much. "Here," I said. "Let me adjust the pillows a little for you. You look like you are sliding down in the bed."

After getting her adjusted, I sat down, and we chatted about her diagnostic tests, who had been to visit, and I finally asked: "Get any calls?"

"Oh, yes," and she rattled off names of family and friends I knew. Then she added with a real smile on her face: "Oh, yes, and I heard from my friend Jo. You must have told her I was in here. Wasn't it nice of her to call with all she has to do and the pain she is in herself?" I thought I would cry on the spot.

When I think back on these two women—and I often do—I see what true kindness is all about. Janice died long ago. Jo is over ninety now and still complains about her arthritis. In honor of Janice, I now listen quietly to Jo's complaints. It's the kind thing to do.

For Reflection

Let us endeavor to live that when we come to die even the undertaker will be sorry.[31]

—Mark Twain

Kindness is accepting people where they are and offering them an interpersonal place where they can feel cared for and grow, if they are so inclined. Who are the people in your life who have been truly kind to you? In their honor, who are the difficult people in your life to whom you are called to be kinder, without having expectations for appreciation or change?

Spiritual Tenet 18

Spiritual kindness is, at its core, offering people acceptance, as well as a little of our time and attention when they are with us, no matter what their response to us may be.

5. completing the circle of grace:

A Few Concluding Comments

So many people have had difficult things happen to them in life that they can only meet each day with so much hurt and a great deal of unresolved needs. They transfer onto us the lingering effects of these past negative markers, events, and lacks. As a result, we are sometimes viewed with unrealistically great expectations, or with a lot of unwarranted mistrust.

God is not calling us to cure these problems. Only God can do that. We are, however, expected to offer people a chance to experience some of the goodness of God through their contact with us. Will we fail in our efforts to do this? Sometimes. Will we feel guilty or resentful at times when people project onto us needs we can't meet, and then anger or hurt when we pull back because we've erroneously overextended ourselves and promised too much? Probably. But, we still need to do what we can—not just for them, but also for us, because *compassion completes the circle of grace*. Without it, self-knowledge will stagnate, our prayer life will become artificial, and—most importantly—we will miss seeing and hearing those words of God that can only be received when we are in service to others.

For Reflection

Here we are touching the profound spiritual truth that service is an expression of the search for God and not just of the desire to bring about individual or social change. This is open to all sorts of misunderstanding, but its truth is confirmed in the lives of those for whom service is a constant and uninterrupted concern. As long as the help we offer to others is motivated primarily by the changes we may accomplish, our service cannot last long. When results do not appear, when success is absent, when we are no longer liked or praised for what we do, we lose the strength and motivation to continue. When we see nothing but sad, poor, sick, or miserable people who, even after our many attempts to offer help, remain sad, poor, sick, and miserable, then the only reasonable response is to move away in order to prevent ourselves from becoming cynical or depressed. Radical servanthood challenges us, while attempting persistently to overcome poverty, hunger, illness, and any other form of human misery, to reveal the gentle presence of our compassionate God in the midst of our broken world.[32]

—Donald P. McNeil, Douglas A. Morrison,

Henri J.M. Nouwen

What is the most important lesson about being compassionate that you want to remember? How have you "seen God" in your own past acts of compassion? What is the greatest danger you must face in being compassionate? How can you transform this danger into a "friend" (positive lesson) for yourself?

Spiritual Tenet 19

Compassion completes the circle of grace by feeding our prayer life with information that helps us understand ourselves and learn more about God.

In this way, service is not merely our doing things for people to gain either God's approval or their gratitude. It is actually an act of sharing God's life within us so that we in turn can learn more about the mysterious unfolding presence of God. Remember, without compassion we run the danger of our prayer becoming little more than a dialogue with our own narcissistic self.

the transparent soul

A Brief Epilogue

When we are ordinary, we are transparent, simply as God intended us to be. We are free. No longer do we waste energy on trying to be who we are not. Images don't matter. Acceptance, while nice, is not necessary.

When we appreciate our mortality by enjoying the now, we are also free. In those instances we are not tyrannized by the past or preoccupied by a future which may not happen. Rather than worrying, we are simply present in the now.

How can this come about? How can we become more transparent, present to the now, free? What will let us flow better with life so we experience more joy and peace, rather than being seduced by the needs for pleasure or security?

Well, the one answer this book has offered is: a simple, healthy, strong, *real* prayer life.

To develop or renew one's prayer life, attention to our "spiritual attitude" — the way we perceive the world — must be brought more clearly into our level of awareness so we can address and nourish it. "A little rule," in which different types of prayer forms nourish our day, must also be structured. And finally, a sense of commitment to being compassionate is needed; sharing and learning more about God's life in the world is not a nicety in the spiritual life — it is a necessity!

In attending to one's *spiritual attitude*, forming *a little rule*, and being *compassionate* in the world, no longer do we need to be constantly captured by worries or feel permanently lost. Instead, as spiritual wisdom teaches us, we will no longer identify with the clouds of life. Instead, we will become "the sky." And so, while the clouds (life's normal pains) will continue to appear, they will eventually pass and the troubles, instead of just being annoying, will also teach us about the love of God as much as the sun of good fortune does. Truly, a life of prayer will allow us to live more fully until the time comes to die. And, what more can we ask than this?

creating a simple, strong prayer life

Common Questions on Forming
"A Little Spiritual Rule"

Structuring "a little rule" to follow in an attempt to ensure we have a more intelligent, fruitful prayer life is simple, but not easy. The following are some ideas in response to a series of questions on forming a little rule, so that our day and life become full and well-lived.

What do you mean by "a little spiritual rule" and why should I bother to develop one for myself?

A little rule is a structure we have for our intentional relationship with God each day. The importance in being clear about ways to pray and to be prayerful is that it provides an *explicit* framework and discipline. In this way, our sense of what is important in life is not inadvertently overwhelmed by being absorbed into, and swept away by, the day's hectic schedule. Instead, "a little rule" helps us to be centered when we enter the day. In addition, it helps us to see each of our gifts, challenges, and conflicts in light of our spiritual values and from a place of inner peace. This does not lead to less pain in life; to expect that would be foolish. But it does help us learn and grow from the necessary pain we encounter in life. Also, it lessens the unnecessary suffering we cause ourselves when we lose sight of God's love for us. In essence then, "a little rule" helps us stay balanced and not lose perspective as often.

What is the first step I should take in developing a structured prayer life?
You probably have already taken that step, namely, joining with others in formal prayer or community worship. If you are not already involved in weekly public worship, you should consider this an important cornerstone of the prayer life. When in prayer together, as a community, we draw strength not just from God but also from each other. We recognize we are not alone, and being with others encourages us in our individual spiritual practices.

Without public worship we can easily lose heart or get off into our own world. When this occurs we will mistake thinking in quiet for meditation and mistake simply being alone with ourselves for being prayerfully in solitude with God.

What would be another important initial step in forming "a little rule"?

Time in silence and solitude, wrapped in gratitude, is the other necessary key of a sound prayer life. To do this, find a quiet place to meditate/pray. It may be a corner of a room or a separate place which you will use for prayer each day. Two to twenty minutes in the morning and ten or twenty minutes in the evening would be a good start. Praying longer is fine, but consistency is better. Even if you're late in the morning, two minutes to center your heart as you enter the day and a few minutes to relax your soul before sleep are essential.

I get confused about what I should do during the quiet time. Is there a basic way to be in silence and solitude that I can fall back on if I get lost?

There are many ways to meditate or pray in quiet. (See Anthony de Mello's *Sadhana* and Ram Dass' *Journey of Awakening* for ideas on prayer forms and approaches to meditation.) However, there are a few basics to remember.

Sit comfortably with your back straight and your hands on your lap.

Breathe easily and deeply through your nose.

Let your thoughts move through you like a train. Don't stop or get on any car that passes. If the same one keeps coming around, place it in the hands of God, and let it go.

Use a one-word mantra (love, Jesus, kindness . . .) to center your heart.

If you get distracted or lost, don't give it much concern. Just use the mantra again or simply pay attention to your breathing to get back on track.

In addition to public worship and prayer/meditation in silence and solitude, in a simple way how do I fit in the other suggestions you have made in the book?

Each week add another element to strengthen the structure of your prayer life so that you don't overburden yourself or make your spiritual life into an artificially designed one. Add those things that will both make you sensitive to God and to mercy, justice, and goodness in others. Some of those elements are:

Taking a few deep breaths prior to making a phone call, visiting someone, or doing a task. During these breaths reflect on God's love for you.

Quietly converse with God during the day using the guidelines offered earlier in this book.

Read sacred scripture and spirituality books to nourish your soul.

Make and build up a network of friends who are also interested in their prayer lives and spiritual practice.

Reflect on the question: How do people feel when they are with me? This is a way of being sensitive to your spiritual attitude and compassion in daily life.

Use a journal to keep some notes on the daily/weekly events and feelings which comprise your spiritual life.

Should I get guidance in structuring and keeping my little rule vital and balanced?

Yes. If at all possible, a spiritual guide who is wiser and holier than you would be a wonderful way to gain support, direction, and to prevent taking extreme or unnecessary steps in your prayer life.

How do I find such a guide?

Ask your spiritual/religious faith group or respected friends who are in guidance themselves for suggestions.

If I don't presently have a guide or director, are there ways to tell if my prayer life is not healthy or balanced?

One way is by looking at "the fruits." Are you moody, under stress when you pray, anxious about what you feel you are being called to do, or depressed by what seems to be coming up in prayer? Negative emotions like that *usually* don't come from God, but instead from our interpretation of what we feel God is saying to us. It is our heavy conscience, our archaic superego speaking, not God. Spiritual guidance is recommended to move us away from the punitive god in our minds to the living God who loves us and calls us to be all we can be by recognizing the loving grace that we are offered unconditionally.

relaxing with god

In this brief book, I wanted to spur some serious thinking on what it means concretely to structure and live a life of prayer. After reading this book through quickly the first time and rereading it slowly a second, a final step designed to help firm up a sense of what it means to be *transparent* (nondefensively open to the gestures of God in life) is to take a line or two on which to reflect, question ourselves about, and pray over, each day. They should also help us to learn how to become intimate with and *relax with God*.

The nice thing about following this approach is that although the process will merely take a few minutes each day—only one hour or so over a period of a month—many of the basic themes of spiritual perspective will have an opportunity to take root and bear good fruit over a period of time. Some of these points may not turn out initially to be meaningful. Others may be of only short-term value. Some, hopefully, will prove of lasting use. However, by approaching the material in this way, you will have given prayerful awareness ("sensing the gestures of God") a higher profile in your outlook on life.

The concluding step to this process, after having finished a month of scattered minutes of reflection, is to take a few more minutes to discover what overall psychological-spiritual theme or paradigm you yourself have come up with in how you wish to lead a life of psychological and spiritual vitality. In other words, what one or two sentences seem to sum up the lessons you have learned about searching for and living a deeply prayerful life? What one phrase might easily help you to recall the presence of God in your life and quickly bring to mind a healthy attitude in how to approach life—especially in difficult or confusing circumstances? What is the spiritual philosophy you have at the source of your own structure ("little rule") for living life more completely and spiritually? I think even the search for this one or two lines will be a rich experience for you. Some extra space is provided after each day for your own thoughts.

a month of
reflections, questions,
suggestions, and
prayers

Day 1

"Looking for God in prayer is like looking for a path in a field of untrodden snow. Walk across the snow and there is your path" (Thomas Merton). Our prayer sometimes may feel awkward, uninspiring, or flat. This is not a problem unless we make it one and then become overly discouraged. Expect and accept that our prayer will not be as we fantasize it should be, and soon our unique relationship with God will develop into a rich and *real* one.

Day 2

Seeking clarity in our understanding of how we should live the spiritual life is one way to kneel before the mystery and darkness of God. Each day be more and more *intrigued* about your spiritual attitude or outlook, the times and ways you pray, and how you are naturally compassionate with your friends, family, and those you meet each day. Be as clear about your talents as your faults; such clarity before the living God will help you to do your part in the spiritual relationship with the divine.

Day 3

True ordinariness is tangible holiness. Find your own identity — the one given you by God, and then seek to be this same person with *everyone*.

Day 4

When we let our defenses down, we become "transparent" so the Spirit of God can be both received and shared through us. How would being transparent change the way you are with people?

Day 5

A spiritual attitude "softens the soul." What will this mean for me today? What do I find are the best ways to open myself up to the surprising presence of God—even in the people and activities with which I am familiar?

Day 6

When autonomy (our will) and theonomy (God's will) intersect and are one, we are truly free. What are those things in my life which are taking away my freedom to simply flow with life? How and why am I giving away this power?

Day 7

"Courage comes and goes. Hold on for the next supply" (Thomas Merton). Lord, let me hold these two sentences in my heart so when I am feeling down or lost, in darkness, challenged or misunderstood, I don't quickly lose heart. Amen.

Day 8

"Pray always and [do] not . . . lose heart" (Luke 18:1). What are those areas in my life that require the greatest perseverance?

Day 9

"I never asked God for success. I only asked for wonder and God gave it to me" (Abraham Joshua Heschel). How can I have low expectation and high hopes? How can I open myself to understand and do God's will and not just simply pray that God does my will?

Day 10

"The contemplative is not the one who prepares his mind for a particular message . . . but [someone] who remains empty" (Thomas Merton). As I sit in prayer with you, Lord, help me not to look for you in a particular way. Help me not to simply seek answers from you or for you to meet the needs that I perceive I have, but to let you reveal yourself to me in your own surprising way. Amen.

Day 11

"Where your treasure is your heart is" (Matthew 6:21). What is it that stirs up the most emotion—both positive and negative—in me? How can I pray about these "idols" in my life so I can enjoy life without so much grasping or fear of losing the gifts I now have?

Day 12

"I know the sunsets are for everyone. But as in observing other works of art, what each of us receives from them are personal gifts from God. They are uniquely ours" (Michaele Aileen Wicks). Find the gift God is offering you in every encounter with people, your work, nature, everything. Although you may not see the grace every time, you will more and more be sensitive to what you are being given by God.

Day 13

A sense of entitlement is one of the major enemies of the spiritual life. Instead of asking, "Am I getting what I desire or feel I should get?" ask, "Am I enjoying to the fullest what is already in my life?"

Day 14

Receive, don't take. What will help me be more deeply grateful so that I am open enough to receive what I am being given in so many different (and sometimes mundane) ways by God?

Day 15

"Happiness can only be felt if you don't set any conditions" (Artur Rubenstein).

Day 16

"Holy remembering" involves recalling the past moments of epiphany (dramatic awakening) in our lives so we can muster the courage and perspective to continue to seek God. Build on your past infatuation with God and life by bringing forth the openness and spiritual passion of the earlier years of life.

Day 17

"You must build your life as if it
were a work of art" (Abraham
Joshua Heschel).
What work of art are you?
How are you appreciating, sharing,
or defacing this "art of God" now?

Day 18

"If in the last few years you haven't discarded a major opinion or acquired a new one, check your pulse. You may be dead" (Gelett Burgess).

Day 19

When I look at the three themes of *spiritual attitude*, *prayerfulness*, and *compassion*, how do I feel they are in balance in my life? Which one needs more attention? Other than the excuse "I'm too busy," what do you think are the reasons this particular area is not getting the attention it deserves?

Day 20

Reflect again on the following
three questions posited at the
beginning of this book:
How do people feel when they
are with me?
Am I really awake, aware,
present to God in my life now?
What does my daily behavior
say about the person I really am?

Day 21

When I feel alone, vulnerable, alienated, or misunderstood, how do I find God *within* these experiences?

Day 22

How am I finding times and periods of silent reflection during the day? What can I do to make such periods more important and attractive so they are not merely other things to do? Instead, how do I make them places I look forward to so I can relax with God in peace and love?

Day 23

What are the most intriguing things about my conversations with God? What are the issues, fears, joys, pleasures, anger, and troubles in my life now? How am I sharing them with the Lord? Am I writing down such thoughts as well so I can see how God and I are relating with each other about them?

Day 24

What place does sacred scripture play now in my life? How can I incorporate scripture in a way that it helps me center my life and enables God to be more real to me, rather than having the reading become another chore?

Day 25

Who are the people in my
(informal and formal) faith-sharing
groups? Who among them are
really important to me now? Why
are they so important?

Day 26

If I was asked to describe my "little spiritual rule" for others, what would be the main structure of it?

Day 27

"It's in the shelter of each other that the people live" (Irish proverb). How am I integrating my search for spiritual wisdom and the desire to share this through compassionate living with others (my family, friends, co-workers, people I meet in passing each day, those I speak to over the phone . . .)?

Day 28

"I have spread my dream under your feet: tread softly because you tread on my dreams" (W. B. Yeats). What are some of the ways you seek to offer gentle space to others in your life? How are you offering yourself the same space?

Day 29

Who are the toughest type of people for you to be compassionate with? Name the people in your life now who fit into this category. How are you interacting with these people in a way which, while seemingly not producing much positive reaction on their part, is still something you feel is good? What other little steps can you take to continue this compassionate action?

Day 30

What is the hardest part for you to embrace in living a peaceful, vibrant, real spiritual life? How can you make this difficulty an ally in your daily search for God?

Summary Theme

What is the spiritual theme of
my life?

spiritual tenets

1. We are always blessed.
2. Stay "spiritually awake."
3. Make space in your life.
4. Receive, don't take.
5. Being in spiritual covenant requires that we remember God's faithfulness so we don't ignore our need for loyalty.
6. We are God's works of art.
7. Becoming disgusted with how you worry about the past and how you are preoccupied with the future is good—it convinces you to let go and enjoy "the now."
8. Seek to be ordinary, transparent, simply the person God created you to be.
9. Each day move to a refreshing and renewing place within, a place where you are in silence, solitude, and wrapped in gratitude.
10. Converse honestly, openly, and often with God each day.

11. Sacred scripture breaks the chains of contemporary thinking, so we must read it as often as possible with a sense of spiritual freshness.

12. We need a faith community of friends to inspire, challenge, tease, and call us to be all we can be without unduly embarrassing us for being where we are now.

13. Absorb good messages from sacred scripture, spirituality books and other types of reading.

14. To have our spiritual life give structure to our day, we need to develop "a little rule" of prayer and reflection.

15. Living nobly is not just a worthy goal, it is an act of worshipping the God who created us to present divine goodness where everyone can take heart from it.

16. Offering balm for tears in the souls of others as a way of making God's gentle presence known in the world requires us to remember two important elements: our limits and our need to be faithful no matter what the results.

17. Real hospitality is not merely being nice to people we don't know; it is welcoming them into our "home-with-God"

through gestures which help them to find the divine presence in their own lives.

18. Spiritual kindness is, at its core, offering people acceptance, as well as a little of our time and attention when they are with us, no matter what their response to us may be.

19. Compassion completes the circle of grace by feeding our prayer life with information that helps us understand ourselves and learn more about God.

books on the spiritual life

Bloom, Anthony. *Beginning to Pray.* Mahwah, NJ: Paulist Press, 1970.

Brother Lawrence. *The Practice of the Presence of God.* Translated by John J. Delaney. New York: Doubleday, 1973.

Dass, Ram. *Journey of Awakening.* New York: Bantam, 1978.

de Caussade, Jean-Pierre. *Abandonment to Divine Providence.* New York: Doubleday, 1975.

de Mello, Anthony. *One Minute Wisdom.* New York: Doubleday, 1986.

_____ . *Sadhana.* New York: Doubleday, 1984.

de Sales, St. Francis. *Introduction to the Devout Life.* New York: Doubleday, 1950.

Hanh, Thich Nhat. *The Miracle of Mindfulness.* Boston: Beacon, 1975.

Harvey, Andrew. *Journey in Ladakh.* Boston: Houghton-Mifflin, 1983.

Heschel, Abraham Joshua. *I Asked for Wonder.* Edited by Samuel Dresner. New York: Crossroad, 1986.

Kornfield, Jack. *A Path With Heart.* New York: Bantam Books, 1993.

Johnston, William, Ed. *The Cloud of Unknowing.* New York: Doubleday, 1973.

Matthiessen, Peter. *Nine-headed Dragon River.* Boston: Shambala, 1985.

Merton, Thomas. *The Wisdom of the Desert.* New York: New Direction, 1960.

_____. *Contemplative Prayer.* New York: Doubleday, 1968.

Norris, Kathleen. *Dakota: A Spiritual Geography.* Boston: Houghton-Mifflin, 1993.

Nouwen, Henri. *Genesee Diary.* New York: Doubleday, 1976.

_____. *Making All Things New.* San Francisco: Harper Collins, 1981.

_____. *Way of the Heart.* New York: Seabury, 1981.

Pennington, Basil. *Lectio Divina.* New York: Crossroad, 1998.

Rimpoche, Sogyal. *The Tibetan Book of Living and Dying.* San Francisco: Harper, 1992.

Stendl-Rast, David. *Gratefulness.* Mahwah, NJ: Paulist Press, 1984.

Books on the Spiritual Life

Wiesel, Elie. *Souls on Fire.* New York: Simon and
    Schuster, 1972.
Yogananda, Paramahansa. *In the Sanctuary of the
    Soul.* Los Angeles: Self-Realization
    Fellowship, 1998.

endnotes

1. Abraham Joshua Heschel, "On Prayer," *Conservative Judaism*, Vol. XXV, No. 1, 1970, p. 11.
2. Paramahansa Yogananda, *In the Sanctuary of the Soul*, Los Angeles: Self-Realization Fellowship, 1998, p. 43.
3. Thomas Merton, quoted in James Finley, *Merton's Palace of Nowhere*, Notre Dame, IN: Ave Maria Press, 1978, p. 117.
4. Anthony de Mello, *One Minute Wisdom,* New York: Doubleday, 1986, p. 11.
5. Robert J. Wicks, *Touching the Holy*, Notre Dame, IN: Ave Maria Press, 1992, p.13.
6. This story is presented in a slightly different fashion in James Fenhagen's wonderful book *Invitation to Holiness*, Morehouse Publishing, 1991.
7. Thomas Merton, quoted in Michael Mott, *The Seven Mountains of Thomas Merton*, Boston: Houghton-Mifflin, 1984, p. 263.
8. David Stendl-Rast, *Gratefulness*, Mahwah, NJ: Paulist Press, 1984, p. 12.
9. Artur Rubenstein, source unknown.

10. Abraham Joshua Heschel, *Man Is Not Alone*, New York: Farrar, Straus, and Young, 1951, p. 165.

11. Abraham Joshua Heschel, *I Asked for Wonder*, ed. Samuel Dresner, New York: Crossroad, 1986, p. ix.

12. Homily by Cardinal Basil Hume, date unknown.

13. Gelett Burgess, source unknown.

14. Anne Morrow Lindberg, *Gift From the Sea*, New York: Pantheon Books, 1991, p. 32.

15. Abraham Joshua Heschel, *I Asked for Wonder*, p. vii.

16. Thomas Merton, source unknown.

17. Henri Nouwen, *The Genesse Diary*, New York: Doubleday, 1976, p. 140.

18. Paramahansa Yogananda, *In the Sanctuary of the Soul*, p. 17.

19. Abraham Joshua Heschel, *God in Search of Man*, New York: Farrar, Straus and Giroux, 1955, p. 238.

20. Henri Nouwen, *Making All Things New*, San Francisco: Harper and Row, 1981, p. 33.

21. Matina S. Horner, "Introduction to the Radcliffe Biography Series," in Robert Coles, *Dorothy Day*, Reading, MA: Addison, Welsey, 1987, p. ix.

22. Thomas Merton, *Contemplative Prayer*, New York: Doubleday, 1968, p. 71.

Endnotes

23. Story about Henri Nouwen told by Joseph Gallagher, Baltimore, MD. Version cited is from *National Catholic Reporter*, Nov. 15, 1996, p. 11.

24. Karl Rahner, source unknown.

25. Abraham Joshua Heschel, *Who Is Man?*, Stanford, California: Stanford University Press, 1965, p. 52.

26. Dr. Collins quoted in Robert J. Wicks, *Seeds of Sensitivity,* Notre Dame, IN: Ave Maria Press, p. 35.

27. Abraham Joshua Heschel, *Jewish Heritage*, Vol. 14, No. 2, Summer 1972, p. 5.

28. W. B. Yeats, source unknown.

29. Thomas Merton, quoted in *The Seven Mountains of Thomas Merton*, p. 405.

30. Henri Nouwen, source unknown.

31. Mark Twain, source unknown.

32. Donald P. McNeil, Douglas A. Morrison, and Henri J. M. Nouwen, *Compassion*, New York: Doubleday, 1982, pp. 31, 32.

Robert Wicks

Robert Wicks helps the helpers "in integrating the psychological and the spiritual so people can extend their emotional flames to others without burning out in the process." Wicks, a professor and chairperson of the graduate programs in pastoral counseling at Loyola College, Baltimore, ministers to relief workers around the world — including those evacuated to the United States from Rwanda during its recent civil war. Wicks is the author of more than 30 books including *Touching the Holy: Ordinariness, Self-Esteem, and Friendship*, *After 50: Spiritually Embracing Your Own Wisdom Years* and *Riding the Dragon: 10 Lessons for Inner Strength in Challenging Times*. He lives with his wife, Michaele, in suburban Baltimore.